PATRIARCHY BLUES

PATRIARCHY BLUES

reflections on manhood

FREDERICK JOSEPH

HARPER PERENNIAL

NEW YORK • LONDON • TORONTO • SYDNEY • NEW DELHI • AUCKLAND

HARPER ● PERENNIAL

FIRST EDITION

Designed by Jen Overstreet
Title page image © Shutterstock, Ton Photographer 4289

Library of Congress Cataloging-in-Publication Data has been applied for.

ISBN 978-0-06-313832-2

22 23 24 25 26 LSC 10 9 8 7 6 5 4 3 2 1

To everyone who has been made to feel as if their nuance is a nuisance.

And to those picking up the pieces others thought they had broken beyond repair.

CONTENTS

MERCY, MERCY ME

To all of those in the process of evolving into someone freer:

For a long time, I thought joy was something I didn't deserve because my cup always seemed to runneth over with pain. So much so that it spilled out into a river of harm I have inflicted on others. But I met joy for the first time a few years ago as I stood on the edge of that river ready to jump in and be swept away.

As I readied myself to jump, suddenly the sun's warmth seemed to drape over and calm me, like a parent's embrace and kiss on the forehead to calm a child. Then the wind whispered in my ears as it pushed me away from that river, "You are more than the trauma you have endured, and you can be more than the trauma you have caused."

I began to cry as I had never cried before, and on that river, I was reborn with the understanding that healing and accountability give us the opportunity to no longer be bound to our past selves.

I am not my past selves.

That day, I believe I was given an assignment, not to simply write a book but rather to create a space. Somewhere we can leave the pieces of ourselves that don't serve joy. Somewhere we can be accountable for who we have been within the oppressive systems that have gaslighted us into being less than who we truly are. Somewhere we can grow and help others feel safe.

The words on these pages sing the song of goodbye to the men I have been and welcome with open arms the man I am becoming. But there is room here for you as well—there is room for all of us.

My love grows daily for the man I am trying to be, but the journey to become him is difficult and I know it will take the rest of my life. As will the work of unpacking how patriarchy, white supremacy, and capitalism have consorted to destroy all we hold dear.

This book is not a map for the journey, but rather a prospective on which direction to go and someone to walk with along the way. I hope that my experiences, my pain, my growth serve as reminders that we are not bound to the gravity of pain. We are not bound to misogyny, homophobia, transphobia, or any manifestation of what has kept us from the ultimate joy of freedom.

May in this space we find strength, understanding, progress, and joy.

May in this space we find the courage to heal and grow.

May in this space we find the warmth of the sun and the honesty of the wind.

With Love,
Fred

INTRODUCTION

A LEGACY OF ANTI-PATRIARCHY

I don't have a good memory. I'm not someone who recalls faces easily or where I might have met you the first time. But it's not for a lack of trying. I dread the moments in which I may accidentally make someone feel as if they were irrelevant to me, or that I don't remember them because I've deemed myself more important than they are. In reality, for quite some time, I've found nearly every interaction I have and person I meet to be important. But I didn't always feel this way.

It wasn't until I was around twenty-four years old that I began to realize how crucial it is to breathe in all parts of those around us, good or bad. How essential it is to grasp the moments of our lives, fleeting or persistent. Connection is one of the most beautiful aspects of being here, and in a terrible turn of fate, I was made to realize this more fully than ever before. After a long stretch of arduous symptoms, I found out my short-term memory loss, along with many other newly developed ailments, was due to me having multiple sclerosis, a diagnosis that would change *everything*. I could no longer grasp anything or anyone as tightly as before, when I didn't even realize how important it was to do so. Suddenly, it felt like my entire life was going to slip away, like trying to clench the last days of summer's sand in your hand.

Learning about my sickness was the first time I considered that at such a young age I could be taken from this world by something other than a white man's rage or a white woman's tears. I spent most of my life being reminded by white supremacy that time is a luxury, but I couldn't reconcile how little of it I might have.

When I was a young boy, teachers often asked me what I wanted to be when I grew up, to which I'd typically respond in a way that would make us both comfortable: "I want to be the president!" As I became older, the answer evolved into things that were more feasible: "I want to be a lawyer." But the truth is that since I was about ten years old all I actually wanted to be when I grew up was alive.

For me at just twenty-four, every moment suddenly felt as though it was borrowed time. Doctors couldn't tell me whether my sickness would become worse or regress back into whatever chasm it came from. All I knew was that this creature lurked in my body and threatened to take everything from me.

But as I saw my mortality looking back at me in the mirror, I began to consider not only the time that I was potentially going to lose—but also the time that I had been given. Who had I been? What would I be remembered for? What would I be remembered as? When I assessed honestly who I had been throughout my life, I didn't like the truth. I had spent most of my youth navigating the world and the people around me through a misogynistic and toxic masculine lens; destroying many of my relationships with others, especially women; and completely failing to reciprocate any semblance of love or respect as I was receiving it. I took those truths and built a boat so that I could sail away and lose myself on an ocean of brown depression, looking for answers at the bottom of the bottle. It's a difficult thing to accept that you may be remembered for more harm than good.

But somewhere along the way I found myself washed up on a shore in the form of a simple truth that was greater than any of my failures. Time is only what you make it. When I reached that shore, I asked myself a question, "Are you willing to try and give more than you have taken?" Since then, my work, including this book, has been an attempt to answer that question.

If there is a devil, he toils in keeping us fixated on our pain rather than on the pain we are causing. But what if together we dared to imagine ourselves beyond the harm we have felt and the harm we have inflicted? I'm daring to imagine all those things.

We will all be called home by our ancestors at some point, that is inevitable. But the question is whether you'll be greeted fondly for what you did while you were away from home.

Realizing your life won't last forever has a way of reminding you to be free. Realizing your name *may* last forever has a way of reminding you to help free others.

As I said, being a Black man in America, I've thought about the concept of freedom since I was very young. Who is free, who isn't free, is anyone free? But for the first time, it dawned on me after finding out I'm sick that I may never get to see any semblance of freedom for myself during my remaining years. That doesn't mean I can't help others have what I never will in this life.

I have never had more conversations about freedom and the work necessary to attain it than during 2020, a year in which the world faced one of the deadliest health crises in history and its subsequent systemic impact. An impact that disproportionately decimated already marginalized communities globally, as is sadly always the case.

It was also a year in which many people believe the world began a long overdue reckoning with both white supremacy and its manifestations, such as police brutality. Personally, I believe we are heading in the right direction, but I don't think we've reached a true reckoning yet. That would require a dismantling of oppressive systems and accountability for the conscious and unconscious roles we all play in them. If a true reckoning was taking place, conversations and policies focused on supporting Black transgender women and reparations would not still be widely framed as "radical."

As I watched the names of Breonna Taylor, George Floyd, Ahmaud Arbery, and many others *rightfully* highlighted across various forms of media, I also saw growth in support for progressive movements and conversations. "Listen to Black women," Black Lives Matter, the importance of Black joy, and Defund the Police were all gaining steam, even if only to regress mightily later on.

The ranks of the *anti-racist* movement were seemingly growing by the day. But I rarely saw mainstream conversations about the record number of trans women who had been murdered, the skyrocketing rates of domestic violence since people spent more time at home together, the assault on reproductive rights throughout the country, and the fact that most of the job loss caused by the pandemic had been suffered by women of color. The failure of many people's anti-racism work is that they don't account for the patriarchy and how it's conditioned us to uphold not only homophobia, misogyny, and transphobia—but white supremacy as well.

Intersectional oppression requires intersectional liberation.

I have spent years coming face to face with and reconciling how I have been conditioned in, complicit with, and upholding of the oppression of others. That is not to say I now think of myself as perfect or some sort of savior. I'm still unpacking what I have sowed in this world. I am working every day to emancipate myself and others from the patriarchy. Because, unbeknownst to those who can't see the chains, we are not nearly close to being free.

As bell hooks said:

Visionary feminism is a wise and loving politics. It is rooted in the love of male and female being, refusing to privilege one over the other. The soul of feminist politics is the commitment to ending patriarchal domination of women and men, girls and boys. Love cannot exist in any relationship that is based on domination and coercion. Males cannot love themselves in patriarchal culture if their very self-definition relies on submission to patriarchal rules. When men embrace feminist thinking and practice, which emphasizes the value of mutual growth and self-actualization in all relationships, their emotional well-being will be enhanced. A genuine feminist politics always brings us from bondage to freedom, from lovelessness to loving.

We are quite literally in a fight for our lives. My hope is that the next generations remember ours as one that held ourselves accountable and fought for each other's lives, and that the children I hope to have one day will be proud that I gave them and myself a chance at being the best versions of ourselves.

LAY OF THE LAND

THE SHORE

Each one of us is a part of someone's ocean of memories. The question is whether we're remembered as someone who helped them float—or tried to sink them.

"Nobody's free until everybody's free."

That quote by the great Fannie Lou Hamer not only changed my life—but also probably saved my soul. Over the past few years, it has been the most important lesson I've learned. Liberation is a lie unless every shackled soul one day finds themselves on the shores of freedom.

Many view this concept as altruistic. But in order for any of us to be free, we must no longer view the oppressions of other people as problems specific to individual groups, but instead understand that oppression in any form decays the very fabric of our society.

Thinking about the necessity of fellowship in this fight for freedom, I'm reminded of the zebra and the ostrich. Not long ago I learned that zebras have keen eyesight but a poor sense of smell, while ostriches have a keen sense of smell but poor eyesight. In understanding their individual weaknesses and the constant threat of falling prey to one of the many predators on the savanna, they often stay close to use the other's strength to help them survive.

What's important is not their differences, but rather their common interests. Together they have a better chance to survive. I think about this often because so many people believe fighting for those they deem different from themselves is an unnecessary act of selflessness. But in many ways our society is not unlike the savanna.

How can any of us truly enjoy breathing in the air of the free while our brothers and sisters are drowning at the bottom of an ocean, still shackled by oppression? What's stopping the ocean's tide from rising to our castles of sand and privilege?

These shackles exist both literally and metaphorically, taking many forms. Their names are widely known, but their impact is immeasurable. White supremacy, homophobia, transphobia, classism—and patriarchy. While each is insidious in its own right, patriarchy and white supremacy are particularly devastating. Not only do they uphold and protect the other oppressive forces, but they are also at the root of almost every facet of our society.

When trying to explain how ingrained patriarchy and white supremacy are in our daily lives, I often find myself using the film *The Matrix* to help peel back the harsh layers of our existence. It is the story of the prodigal savior Neo, a person who takes a red pill and learns that everything he knows and loves about the world is a fabrication used to manipulate humans into serving robots. He must then decide whether he is going to tear the system down and lose his privileges and way of life in that system or return to the façade.

While we've yet to be enslaved by our MacBooks and iPhones (at least not literally), the film serves as a perfect critique of society's constructs and power dynamics. And it keenly identifies the dilemma that people who benefit from the systemic oppression of other people often face.

White supremacy and patriarchy function much like the computer-generated world in the film, a reality composed of binaries: right and wrong, haves and have-nots, man and woman. A blueprint that influences everything you and I do, wear, think, and even how we treat one another, whether we realize it or not.

I was about eight years old when I started playing an active role in upholding the patriarchy. It was a simple, yet telling moment. I hid the fact that I enjoyed watching musicals, such as *West Side Story*, from my classmates because during lunch I overheard one of them say musicals were "gay." Like me, I'm sure my classmate had no idea what "gay" meant. He likely heard it from one of his parents, at church, or on television. Regardless, we all knew it was something bad that none of us wanted to be.

The reality is that for me, hiding my love for musicals was merely an attempt to avoid ridicule, but for others, it can be a matter of avoiding life-threatening situations. Hiding is something that millions of people do to simply survive; these people are often forced to hide their whole selves from the world for safety because they don't fit into the boxes designated for them. Boxes for their interests, boxes for their gender, boxes for who they are allowed to be.

After that moment, I spent most of my life stumbling through a jungle of misogyny and sexism, which I'm still navigating my way out of now. But until a few years ago, I didn't even know I was lost.

On the other hand, my history with white supremacy is completely different from my history with homophobia, as I've considered it in everything I do since childhood. I thought about it more than sleeping, eating, or breathing. As an eight-year-old, I may not have known it was wrong to call things "gay," but I certainly knew what a "nigger" was.

While thinking about white supremacy has helped keep me alive, I often envy those who don't carry the same burden. Whether they are white and don't want to be held accountable for how they benefit from this system or they are non-white and living in blissful and deadly ignorance—I often envy them. In fact, I envy them so much, sometimes I hate them.

I hate them for not helping cut down the trees from which we are lynched, for their hearts not racing when a police car rolls by, for not being disrespected by white women who clutch their purses when we are near.

I hate them for not taking the red pill—for being complicit.

Over the past few years, the term "anti-racism," which means an active role in dismantling racist systems, has become popularized. It's the idea that, basically, it's no longer enough to simply not be racist. If you're against racism you should be doing things to end it. And I agree.

But how then do I reconcile my existence within a society in which the power and privilege that come from marginalizing others belongs not only to those who are white, but also to those who are cisgender heterosexual men?

Men such as myself.

How can I sit idly as we continue to murder and wage war against my brothers' and sisters' rights to marry, make reproductive choices, and just—be?

If I expect white people to actively participate in destroying white supremacy because they possess the power within this system, I'd be a hypocrite to not expect the same of myself regarding the patriarchy and everything that falls under it.

I'd be a hypocrite to not join the ranks of the anti-patriarchy.

Thankfully, I was eventually offered my own red pill. And just in time for a potential renaissance of progressivism and empowerment that could see the scales of equality tipping toward the marginalized. But as is always the case with progress, there are those who will do anything to stop it.

Stopping it may be an understatement, as the world is in the middle of the greatest identity crisis in society's history. The advent of the internet and popularization of social media have birthed global communities that have helped usher in an era of understanding and education amongst people from various walks of life. But it's also provided refuge and a strategic base for those who find community in keeping others oppressed.

As a cisgender heterosexual man, I belong to the group that has created and perpetrated these oppressive behaviors and systems. Therefore, it is largely up to us to help destroy them. But it's not enough to simply pick up a weapon; we should be locking arms with our sisters on the front lines.

We must all play a role in defeating a monster into which we all continue to breathe life in our own ways. Which is why it's important that our conversations about how we got here and where we are going be nuanced and intersectional.

As I reflect upon how I became so lost, I wish I could blame my problematic history and absence from the front lines of this fight solely on the men in my life who taught me their problematic behaviors—but none of them were around to do so. Nearly everything I learned about being a man, whether right or wrong, was taught to me by society at large and validated by the women around me. Like white supremacy, the patriarchy is at its strongest when its victims are unknowingly upholding it.

I'm of the belief that a rising tide lifts all ships, and in my opinion, as the most marginalized group in society, Black people are the tide for both white supremacy and patriarchy. Therefore, a society in which Black people are free is a society in which all oppressed people are free. Over the years I have learned that freeing all Black people is best accomplished by centering the liberation of the most marginalized in our community—cis and transgender Black women.

We have glorified and rewarded the exploitation, perversion, and limitations of anyone who is not a cisgender heterosexual man. This is the greatest, and most dangerous, expression of how deep the roots of patriarchy and white supremacy go.

Our current conception of manhood has become a prison for so many, and unless we seriously reevaluate it, it will be the end of us all.

PATRIARCHY IS . . .

The man said he treats women fairly so patriarchy has nothing to do with him . . .

The woman said patriarchy was only something the man does . . .

The son said he didn't experience patriarchy because his mother held all the power . . .

The daughter said her sister had been born her brother and she didn't experience true patriarchy . . .

The grandfather said women had gained their rights so patriarchy didn't exist . . .

The grandmother agreed with the grandfather . . .

They were all wrong.

I added my pronouns (he/him) to my social media bios a few months ago. Shortly after, I received countless messages calling me "soft," accusing me of supporting a "gay agenda," and other things I'm not going to repeat. I wasn't necessarily surprised by the messages, as they were fairly tame compared to what I often receive. But I was surprised by *who* the messages were from.

As I combed through the bombardment of DMs from bigoted men (occasionally stopping to laugh at the young white men who were seemingly still in high school yet insisting I "understand nothing about the world around me"), I noticed quite a few women had messaged me as well. I wasn't really surprised by the fact that women were holding problematic views. But I was surprised that based on their bios, most of these women claimed to be feminists or progressives, or to have some liberal alignment.

I responded to a few of the messages, asking these women why they were actively upholding the patriarchy, to which most replied that they weren't. Most responses I received were some variation of "The patriarchy is about men oppressing women."

As I was working on this book I thought about these responses and people's limited view of the patriarchy, and how, funnily enough, the patriarchy was designed to limit their view. It was a keen reminder of how oppressive systems and beliefs are so ingrained in our culture that people often don't understand or agree upon what constitutes them. For many, concepts such as *patriarchy* have been part of the zeitgeist and cultural lexicon for generations. For others they are just being introduced. Either way, the work of defining these words is deeply important, as doing so often reveals how insidious these systems are. Which is why I felt defining my sense of the patriarchy and its manifestations was a necessary place to start.

First, I must admit that for some time, I considered patriarchy solely through the lens of individual men committing acts against individual women or groups of women. But much as with racism, there are various manifestations of the patriarchy, including societal systems and structures each of us exists within. An individualistic lens absolves those who may not be committing conscious or unconscious direct patriarchal acts but still benefit from the structures and systems of the patriarchy.

One of the most destructive aspects of the patriarchy is that in our own ways, we all adhere to it. The people we vote for, the music we listen to, the films we watch, the sports we play, the extent to which we love others and receive love in return. It has all been shaped in some way by the patriarchy.

Another flaw in my lens was that I failed to see how anyone on a spectrum of gender may be indoctrinated, conditioned, and influenced by patriarchal norms. Anyone can uphold the patriarchy, and in many ways, most do. As I was growing up, my aunts would often tell me that I needed to find a woman who could cook, clean, and do other domestic tasks, not realizing that they themselves were minimizing a woman's existence and worth to being able to serve another person, specifically a man. That's what they were taught throughout their lives, and thus those patriarchal standards were normalized. But these toxic standards and gender roles are based not in sensibility, but rather in subjugation. Ironically, my aunts also taught me all the domestic tasks they problematically had assigned to women as a gender norm.

All of that said, from an attempted intersectional and inclusive lens, I define patriarchy as:

The emotional, physical, mental, metaphysical, political, social, and economic manifestation of the false belief and oppressive ideology that individuals and groups aligned with what is subjectively deemed to be femininity and/or womanhood are inferior or of lesser value than the subjective opposite, i.e., masculinity and/or manhood.

These false beliefs and oppressive ideologies are upheld by systems, structures, and behaviors created and designed to overtly and subtly normalize, condition, and indoctrinate both those oppressed for femininity and womanhood and those benefiting from masculinity and manhood. Said systems, structures, and behaviors are aimed at upholding and maintaining power amassed by the benefiting group.

Manifestations of the patriarchy are often about what is perceived as feminine versus masculine, both of which are subjective and may exist within any person, regardless of their gender identity. But the constructed superiority of white men and traditional masculinity has given birth to not only the systems and structures that benefit their creators, but also a fraternal bond between them, a "boys' club" ideology— a toxic culture that thrives on normalizing patriarchal culture in its most overt and oppressive forms. In this way, cisgender (historically heterosexual) men have accumulated power through their systems and structures, to be parsed out and leveraged solely by the people within this club.

Who may or may not gain proximity to this boys' club depends upon what country, community, culture, and era you're referring to, but in the present-day United States, it is made up of mostly those who are cisgender, heterosexual, able-bodied, capitalist, Christian, and white. And no group holds more power or is able to create more opportunities for joining this boys' club than those who fit under one main category: *whiteness*.

ON THE EIGHTH DAY, THE LORD MADE OPPRESSION

Massa Reverend Washington walked through the doors and down the center aisle to the front of the church. Everyone stood to praise him for his graciousness in blessing the lord's house with the good word on that fine Sunday!

"Y'all gon' head and sit down. I want to first lay praise at the feet of his highest, our lord and savior, Jesus Christ. Let the church say amen!"

The church said amen.

"Now before I get started, I want y'all to remember a few things, cause I hear it's been some murmurs of question and doubt. First off, Jesus most certainly was a white man with blue eyes, sort of looked like me, matter fact. All that hair on his head like wool and feet lookin' like bronze glowing in a furnace . . . it's all misunderstood. Again, Jesus was a white man, and it's this very fact that reminds you that I am the closest thing to Jesus you all got. The white man was divinely chosen to lead you out of your wretchedness and away from y'all's false gods. Which is why if I hear any more murmurs of leaving, or praise being laid upon anyone other than myself and Jesus . . . there will be hell to pay. Now let's get to this word to save y'all's souls from misunderstandings."

Amen.

Massa Reverend Washington gave what many thought was the best sermon of his life that day.

My belief is that there is a God, a higher power, and a divine beautiful existence that you may see in the eyes of a child or in the colors of the sky as the sun rises. But I don't conform to or believe in any man-made religion, and I am only now learning to conform to and believe in love—the first religion.

I have no issue with anyone who is religious. In fact, there was a time in which the Baptist church was more of a home to me than my own body. Though we weren't in the pew every Sunday, you wouldn't have known it from the spirit in our lives. Gospel music on weekend mornings and prayers before meals were as essential in my family as water and breathing. But at eighteen, the young man who had once spent summers at Bible camp suffered a crisis of faith.

In April 2007, Thelma Ford died after her second battle with breast cancer, having never told her family about the first. She was my confidant, my best friend, and my grandmother. She didn't tell us she had been sick because she was conditioned to believe in the toxic narrative that she was somehow a *stronger* Black woman for her ability to withstand pain without seeking help. By the time we knew what was happening to her, it was too late.

As I sat less than three feet away from the small wooden box that housed the mortal remains of a woman who was larger than life, anger filled my veins. The reverend presiding over the service had spoken at length about how "good" and "strong" my grandmother was, to which those in the room responded with a resounding "yes, lord!" and "amen!" He then began singing "I Won't Complain" by Reverend Paul Jones as he placed one hand on the small wooden box that was too pedestrian for a queen. Those in the room who knew the lyrics sang along to the song, which reflected a person who is constantly down, distraught, and suffering, but ultimately will not complain—because Jesus is by their side. Not because Jesus will make sure things become easier or their suffering will eventually end, but rather because if he is with you in your struggle, that's all that matters.

It was in that moment that I realized the song was about my grandmother, and the millions of Black people like her. Those born into pain, forced to stumble through a life of struggle, and then broken by the exhaustion of unfairness. All while claiming that Jesus would make a way. He was there as my grandmother lay for weeks in hospice, there in the fields of cotton as my grandmother's grandmother toiled, and in the town square as my great-great-grandfather was strung from a lamppost. He just didn't do anything about it.

I couldn't reconcile how we were praising a father who seemingly loved only some of his children. There was nothing I wanted more in that moment than to stand and reach out for Jesus, grab him by the arm, and force him to look in that small wooden box three feet away. Force him to look upon his complicity—and let him know I was done with him.

As the ground was placed upon my grandmother's casket to close her physical connection to this world, my own understanding of this world was only beginning. I spent the next few years studying theology, trying to better grasp what I had so vehemently believed in my whole life. I began to realize how much of the oppression we were facing was actually rooted in and upheld by Christianity.

This is not to say that Christianity is the only religion that has been used as a tool of oppression. The same is true for all religions. Some by their inherent nature, and others because of their problematic interpretations and/or reimagining by oppressive people with power. But in the context of America, and most of the Western hemisphere, Christianity reigns supreme as a pillar of capitalistic, patriarchal, and white supremacist oppression. All of which we saw on full display with the white Christian evangelical support for Donald Trump in both the 2016 and 2020 elections, though it supersedes those moments. Since the founding of America, Christianity has been used as a tool of oppression, and navigating that reality is a key to dismantling patriarchy.

There is no specific doctrine within Christianity that says women must face the constant wrath of misogyny or sexism, but the hierarchal structures established by both patriarchal culture and Christian doctrine have combined to create inequality and oppression. If the Bible is meant to act as a guideline for behavior and worldview, there are various passages that have overtly canonized patriarchy. One example is 1 Corinthians 11:4–9:

> Every man who prophesies or prays with his head covered brings shame to his head. But every woman who prays or prophesies should have her head covered. If she does not cover her head, she brings shame to her head. Then she is the same as the woman who has her head shaved. If a woman does not cover her head, it is the same as cutting off all her hair. But it is shameful for a woman to cut off all her hair or to shave her head. So she should cover her head. But a man should not cover his head, because he is made like God and is God's glory. But a woman is man's glory. The man did not come from a woman. The woman came from man. And man was not made for a woman. Woman was made for man.

This passage could just as easily read, "Women are less than men, and we should enjoy subjugating them." From a biblical perspective, the inferiority of women can be traced back to the very way mankind came to exist. God made Adam in his image, and Eve was then made from the rib of Adam. The fact that Eve was made from Adam as opposed to also being made directly from God has informed much of the implied hierarchy of men and women we see today, because one may interpret, and many have interpreted, Adam as being closer to God than Eve, and thus more entitled to power.

These Christian themes have led to the abuse and domination of women, as seen with the utter lack of autonomy in the eyes of American law, which has never truly separated church and state. Women's voting rights, reproductive rights, and need to fight for other basic human rights to this day can be traced directly back to how Christian doctrine is woven into the sociopolitical fabric of America.

Two other important common themes throughout the Bible, and specifically in the New Testament, are grace and forgiveness. This idea of "turning the other cheek" as it relates to how one might handle being wronged typically benefits only the wrongdoer, and often absolves those who hold power within Christianity of accountability. These themes are used to condition and gaslight believers to this day to help reinforce and protect the very structures, systems, and people who are oppressing them.

As famed feminist Barbara G. Walker once said, "From the pulpit, men were ordered to beat their wives, and wives to kiss the stick that beat them."

Until a few decades ago, American Christian-centric common law decreed that a husband should have the right to discipline his wife physically. Until it was ruled against in most places, interspousal tort immunity also existed; this principle made it impossible for a wife to succeed in any legal action against her husband or testify against him in a court of law. This combination shielded men from any legal ramifications or public accountability for domestic abuse.

I can't speak to what the Bible was intended to do, that knowledge is buried with its architects. But I do believe the text wasn't meant to be oppressive, but rather to be a body of work that speaks to liberation and morality. In fact, Christianity began as prophetic opposition to oppressive social and political systems of its time. But "morality" and "liberation" are both relative terms, and while the intent of Christianity and its doctrine may have been rooted in liberation, the vantage point of how to build upon this intention solely derives from men's views and beliefs.

Not only was the text of the Bible written by men, but the reading and interpretation has also historically been a role designated primarily to men, and more times than not, cisgender heterosexual white men. This has allowed them to preach and teach a word from the perspective of someone with an agenda often aimed at further bigotry and personal gain.

Again, this is not to say that the nature of Christianity is inherently oppressive, but rather that throughout history, many of the people who have had power within Christianity have knowingly or unknowingly furthered and upheld oppressive ideologies and structures. Especially those rooted in white colonial patriarchy.

There is a conscious effort in many spaces to lean into the most radically liberating aspects of Christianity, but this work is moot without also navigating accountability and accepting the truth that Christian beliefs have constructed and insulated much of the patriarchal oppression many people face. I am glad my grandmother departed this life having faith that there was something more, something better waiting for her upon her arrival at her destination. It's faith that gives us purpose and sense in a life that may be void of both. But the same faith that has kept people hopeful has also played a large part in keeping people chained.

As I've journeyed, stumbled, and fallen in the years since my grandmother left this world, I have found myself lifted once again to and by faith. But not a faith that may be found in religious texts or buildings designated for worship.

I found God again as I sat on a balcony in Stone Town in Zanzibar. The balcony overlooked a beach that extended into a harbor, and on this particular day I sat and watched the scene below until the sun began to set. There was a group of young Tanzanian children kicking a soccer ball to one another as the water washed the sand from their feet.

I admired them for hours as they ran, smiled, and laughed while their Black skin was bathed in the light of the East African sun. I was in awe of how happy they seemed. As the sun kissed the horizon, a few of the children began leaving while others continued to giggle and enjoy something that felt foreign to me. A tear rolled down my cheek. In those hours, in those moments, in that sun, those beautiful Black children were home and carefree. Even if only in that space and time. It was something I had never known or truly seen of Blackness in America, as something destructive always seems to be looming. But there I saw the full potential of Black futures, and as the sun made space for the moon, I realized God had shown me what she looks like.

THE FIRST COLOSSUS

The nicely racist white guy who "loved" the Black man's debut book was shocked by the fact that the Black man had stolen from people and sold drugs to pay for his college applications. He was also amazed by the fact that the Black man had been to a Coinstar more times than he had flown on a plane. But more than anything, he was appalled after hearing that the Black man had been arrested for punching a man who looked like he could be related to the nicely racist white guy.

"I thought you were one of the good ones," said the nicely racist white guy.

Do not judge me,
Do not chastise the sons you wrote from your will,
Your sea-washed, sunset gates stand upon my bones.
Still bearing the scars from birthing this infant,
Still bound by the lashings of your original sin,
Torched our homes, made our mothers exiles.
You lie with testaments and tenements,
I lie in tatters and dilapidation,
Mountains of Black bodies peeking from the air-bridged harbor.
Whether bastard or beast, the empty-bellied share your name,

Whether the hue is to your favor, we too are the heirs of this
  enterprise,
"Lose, ancient land, the mother of us all" smiles she
With cracking whips.
The corrupt father's hue finds him lauded for feeding his family,
The depraved father's hue finds him praised for feeding his greed,
"I am tired, I am poor, still huddled in masses yearning to breathe
  free,
The wretched refuse of liberty's eroding shore.
I have been here, the homeless, tempest-tost be thy name,
Do not judge me as I lift my lamp to enter the broken window,
I have been locked out of the golden door."

FALSE BINARY

They stood up at the podium in front of the entire world and said, "Gender is fake. Sexuality is a spectrum. And I will identify as who I am, not who you can wrap your mind around. Thank you."

They walked offstage and there was a silence. A moment later the liberals and conservatives locked arms and rushed toward the stage to set the podium on fire, hoping to make sure their children weren't next.

My twenties were filled with friends who for the most part didn't hold social or political views that aligned with mine, but I didn't find this out until my thirties. Primarily because my twenties were basically split between an extremely long party and staying up way too late doing last-minute work that I should have been doing while at said party. Neither left much space for truly getting to know the people around me outside the fact that they enjoyed being in loud sweaty places and drinking overpriced well drinks just as much as I did.

But in my thirties those well drinks and clubs have been replaced by weddings, children celebrations, and the occasional group getaway. Not only has each of these been far easier on my body, which can barely take two old-fashioneds these days, but they've also given me a chance to have conversations and truly get to know many of my friends. It's also given me the chance to constantly argue with these friends.

One of those arguments happened recently when a friend invited me to a gender-reveal party for his first child. Historically I've tried my best to avoid gender-reveal parties because frankly I've always found them annoying. Especially since people became so outlandish about them. I mean forest fires have been started to simply let people know the gender of someone's child. It's insufferable.

But over the past few years, my stance against gender reveals has evolved from simply being against their annoyance to focusing on the problematic nature of what they stand for. A gender reveal doesn't just announce gender, it dictates and reaffirms it. Shooting blue smoke out of a prop to announce you're having a boy is the beginning of placing a child in a box of existence that a parent wants for them. Why blue smoke for a boy? Why not pink? Orange is a lovely color, no? Because society has aligned blue with boys, masculinity, and countless other false pretenses about sex and gender.

So when my friend invited me to his party, I told him that I wasn't going to be able to come, not because I was busy, but because it didn't align with my social views. He asked what I meant, and I explained to him that the very concept of a gender reveal erased the existence of people who exist outside of the binary. He frustratedly said, "Not everything has to be a political statement. Some things are just what they are. Nothing behind it."

I told him that I agreed, not everything has to be a political statement, but this wasn't one of those things. Then I made the point that he didn't know his own child yet, and it was unfair for the parents to place the weight of their ideologies on their child. My friend's frustration quickly evolved into anger because of the mere insinuation that his child could be transgender or gender nonconforming. He responded by saying some things that I didn't appreciate and then hanging up, having not at all considered the points I had presented to him. We haven't spoken since, so I suppose I'm not sure whether I should refer to him as a friend. During our conversation he said one thing that stuck with me: "You know I'm a supporter of the LGBTQ community. Love is love. Don't try and make me out to be something I'm not."

People so often legitimize their problematic positions with surface-level allyship, just as often as they acknowledge the humanity of the LGBTQ+ community only through the "Love Is Love" lens, which merely respects people's ability to be romantic rather than respecting their ability to simply exist as who they are.

If you've come here for perspective on why "Love Is Love," you will leave as you came. I'm uninterested in marketing campaigns, or the respectability politics aligned with them, aimed at helping people wrap their minds around who gets to be human. This is an appeal for what is real and a critique of what is not. A reminder that the very nature of something or someone existing makes it worth protecting. In other words, my focus here is that everyone deserves the space to be themselves, especially when being yourself doesn't harm anyone else.

Sir Winston Churchill once said, "History will be kind to me for I intend to write it."

I think about that quote often. I'm sure many believe that he meant it figuratively. As in, he will do things worthy of history considering him fondly. I try not to underestimate the narcissism of powerful white men.

He had the power and status to influence narratives about himself however he saw fit. This isn't a new concept. Historically, whoever owns the books gets to dictate who writes them and what they write about. It's through this influence that we understand villains and heroes, right and wrong, wins and losses. As well as gender identity and sexuality.

For centuries, narratives and storytelling have been controlled by individuals and belief systems rooted in cisgender heteronormative patriarchy. This has led many to believe that queer existences are relatively new, when in fact this couldn't be further from the truth. It is a known fact that queer people have existed as far back as humans can be traced. But as in much of Western history, strategic erasure has greatly changed the story most people know.

During the Nazi reign in Germany, for instance, homosexuality was so vilified that among the first things the Nazi party did when coming into power was burn books that spoke of queerness, dissolve organizations supporting queer lives, and place many Germans deemed homosexual in concentration camps. While some of these acts may seem archaically horrific, they are not unlike actions that have been taken against the queer community globally in recent history. In America, this type of persecution is still all too familiar for those in the queer community, who are just beginning to see some of the gaps in healthcare and human rights closing.

All of that to say, the patriarchy's war on the queer community is not new, and neither is the community itself. We've just been taught that the community is. Part of this belief has been propagated by the false claims that science proves there are only two genders and that homosexuality is a problematic anomaly. Both are lies.

An abundance of studies prove that gender and sexuality exist on a spectrum and the male and female binary we were taught in school is a social construct. But the insidiousness of cisgender heteronormative conditioning is the belief that people in the queer community should prove the legitimacy of their existence. We've developed a culture that forces them to provide evidence to the rest of us that they are somehow more than figments of their own imagination.

I read a comment online recently that said, "Now all of a sudden people are trans." Not only is this transphobic, but it's ahistorical; there are societies thousands of years old that speak to the existence of transgender people. For example, in ancient Greece some priests identified as women and wore what was considered feminine attire; they are widely considered early transgender figures. In African history over twenty tribes have gender transformation beliefs rooted in spirituality and have praised intersexed deities. These are just two examples of how existence outside a binary gender framework isn't a modern construct at all. The modern construct is the expectation that people must conform to a binary.

This fixation on binary has led to the normalization of abuse against the queer community. It exists on many fronts, from legislation such as the trans military ban under the Trump administration to medical discrimination and lack of employment opportunities to targeted online and real-life harassment and attacks. This constant abuse is a major reason for numbers such as these:

- 40% of LGBTQ respondents to a survey by the Trevor Project had seriously considered attempting suicide in the past twelve months, with more than half of transgender and nonbinary youth having seriously considered suicide in 2020.
- 68% of LGBTQ youth reported symptoms of generalized anxiety disorder in the past two weeks, including more than three in four transgender and nonbinary youth in 2020.

It is sad that these disheartening numbers reflect that most people uphold and perpetuate homophobia and transphobia in some way.

Internalized homophobia and transphobia often result in externalized attacks, such as slurs, threats, and violence. Much of that internalization is rooted in gender biases and stereotypes. This exists in some of society's most common practices, such as the gender-reveal parties that I refuse to attend and inter-sex mutilation. If you're unfamiliar with inter-sex mutilation, that is likely because this issue is not often discussed in many spaces, even though roughly 1.7 percent of people are born intersex.

A person who is born intersex has reproductive anatomy and sex traits that don't conform to the socially traditional female or male body. In many cases, doctors and parents decide to "fix" intersex children by operating on them so their bodies conform to more traditional binary standards.

This approach is deeply problematic for a myriad of reasons. Not only do these surgeries carry a great deal of risk, but they are done in an effort to reaffirm the false notion of gender and sex binaries when the existence of a person born intersex inherently disproves this concept. Last, these decisions erase all autonomy, denying that these children deserve to decide one day what is best for themselves and their bodies.

This sort of polarizing of gender through a cisgender heteronormative lens has implications for all of us.

When we preconceive gender identity and sexuality for young people, we ultimately develop toxic constraints for them. This forced alignment with gender and sexuality standards is what teaches women and girls that their duty is to be caretakers and men and boys that their duty is to provide. What encourages boys to venture out and girls to stay close by. Why men are stereotyped as replacing emotions such as sadness or caring with anger and determination, versus women who instead of being cunning and ambitious, are meant to be caring and docile. We steal our children's ability to embody a full range of emotions by gendering emotional expression. Each one of us is angry, sad, anxious, happy, afraid, excited, embarrassed, determined, weary, and so much more.

If a boy is taught at home or in society that boys don't cry, he will become a man who may not believe in empathy or compassion, maybe even see them as weaknesses. Those weaknesses will be replaced by something deemed more appropriate and aligned, such as anger. Girls on the other hand are taught that anger is a less acceptable emotion; therefore they may replace anger with sadness, as a woman's tears are more palatable than a woman's fire. In both cases, children are being hindered.

There are no such things as "masculine" or "feminine" traits; the belief that there is conditioning in patriarchal ideology has stifled generations of people from expressing and embodying their spectrum of emotions. Which has had a catastrophic impact on the world around us. And all these beliefs have created untrue binaries and polarizing cisgender heteronormative character stereotypes that don't allow for individuality. We are limiting who and what our society is or may become.

Sadly, I've lived this binary firsthand. One of the earliest things I can remember being taught by those around me was that boys don't cry. This idea lived in me and grew, or rather festered like a sore. I learned to travel through life without expressing certain emotions, which was supposed to make me a strong and dependable man. But all it did was make me physically, emotionally, and mentally incomplete.

A boy who is taught not to cry is not a better man, he is an emotionally unavailable man, and at worst an apathetic, which is a very dangerous, man.

There are tears that belong to my trauma, my pain, and my loss that never had a chance to flow but instead were dried to the point that healing has often felt like a mirage. A friend of mine was murdered while I was in college, and when I found out I punched at least five holes in a wall near me. Yes, I was angry that I had lost my friend, but I also didn't have access to any other emotion. When his friends and family gathered at his mother's home after his funeral, I stood in a corner balling my fists and thinking about how much I wanted to hurt the people who had taken him from us.

I'd known his mother since we were children, and when she saw me in the corner, she walked over, looked at me for a moment, and said, "You haven't cried once for my son." I simply said, "I'm going to get them back for this." The words left my mouth not just as a statement, but as a promise. I had every intention to harm the people who had murdered him.

She looked me in the eyes, then hugged me tight and said, "A bunch of angry boys who don't know how to cry are the reason my son is dead. More anger and violence won't bring him back. Cry for my son, you both deserve it. Let it out."

The tears that flowed from me then began to change my life. I cried for my friend, I cried over the father who didn't want me, I cried over how hard it was to cry. That was the day I started to truly become a man.

We steal so much from the girl who deserves to be angry, the boy who deserves to be sweet, and the child who wants to be all of it and none of it. The gender reveals and false binary ideals erase not only our possibilities, but our realities. In both, you and I live masculine traits and feminine traits, which are all just human traits. There's no reason for us to be diluting and stifling who we are because others have socialized us into their beliefs about gender identities and sexuality.

Unless we see the world outside a binary lens, we will be breaking the chains of patriarchy only to find ourselves still locked in a cell.

GENERATIONAL CURSES

A bunch of old white men walk into a white house . . .

The first white man, named Thomas Jefferson, tells the group that Black folks were "cursed" with "a very strong and disagreeable odor" and were incapable of producing art and poetry. Then he says Black people should be deported because Black people and whites could not live together peacefully.

They laugh.

The second white man, named Andrew Jackson, tells the group that one of the Black men he enslaved had escaped once and that he offered $50 for the return of him in an 1804 advertisement. He then tells them that he promised an extra $10 "for every hundred lashes any person will give him, to the amount of three hundred." One of the other white men then asks what he thought of abolitionist pamphlets urging for Black people to be free; he simply replies, "Unconstitutional and wicked."

All the men nod in agreement.

The third white man, named Woodrow Wilson, chuckles as he listens to the other men, then describes his time as president of Princeton University, where he worked tirelessly to keep Black people out. The men praise him for his work, so he tells them about how he refused to reverse segregation in civil service. They praise him some more. Woodrow is so pleased with the response, he decides he would celebrate by showing <u>The Birth of a Nation</u> on the White House lawn that week.

The men are excited.

The fourth white man, named Dwight Eisenhower, tells the group that he could not understand why white Southerners have such a bad reputation; he says they "are not bad people. All they are concerned about is that their sweet little girls are not required to sit in school alongside some big overgrown Negroes."

"Not my daughter," all the men think to themselves.

The sixth man, named Lyndon Johnson, looks at Dwight Eisenhower, shakes his head, sighs, and says simply, "Niggers."

The men look at Lyndon Johnson and smile in surprise.

The seventh man, named Richard Nixon, complains about how lazy Black people are: "We're going to place more of these little Negro bastards on the welfare rolls at $2,400 a family . . ."

All the men nod in agreement.

The eighth and final man, named Ronald Reagan, has been listening intently and agreeing with the men. "Gentlemen, I love what you all stand for. But I have a less obvious approach, something a bit more subtle. We're going to bring slavery back, boys!"

Dear Uncle Randall,

When I decided to write this letter, I wondered how best to speak to you, knowing all too well the things you were harboring. I understand the good parts you lost in the storm, as many of mine were lost in that same hurricane. Our decades of distance had both nothing and everything to do with one another. Two men suffering from stolen smiles and stolen time, on land where both were scarce.

The best way of speaking to someone who has fought and lost to the monsters we have is with honesty. Well, honestly, I miss you and wish I'd done this sooner.

I drove up to Albany last weekend to close out your storage unit. Seeing the flowers blooming along the way made it a far more somber ride. I suppose it reminded me that life goes on, regardless who goes on with it. I'm sure you won't love to hear this, but Uncle Mark took the bus from South Carolina to drive upstate with me. I felt it was only right to give him a chance to say goodbye, since I could tell he was beating himself up for never saying "I'm sorry." Honestly, I'm not sure you wanted me to go either, but it needed to get done, and there was no one else to do it.

There were moments over the past few months I swore I was going to find myself on the highway at 7 am, heading to try and puzzle together your life from whatever you left in a 10 x 15 box. But instead, I opted to pay the fees for a few more months, opted to wait before having to both get to know you and let you go at the same time. But eventually always finds us one way or another. So, there we were standing in front of unit 361, the physical accumulation of a life—your life.

The first thing I noticed was how detail oriented you were; every box was labeled and had a very well-thought-out place. We're unlike in that way, I ruined that tidy space pretty quickly.

The more of your boxes we went through, the more demons I could tell Uncle Mark was wrestling with. Each time we found some of your books, CDs, and shirts that might have smelled like you he stepped outside to smoke or to cry. I didn't mind it much. I felt as if you and I were getting to share space alone for the first time. Sad to think that in over thirty years I had never spent time alone with any of my uncles, or any men I share blood with besides my nine-year-old brother.

Every box I opened told a story that revealed a little bit more about you. There were books by Baldwin and Morrison, CDs by Thelonious and Coltrane, and stacks of printed internet research. You were searching for something that we lost so long ago. In that way, we were more alike than either of us knew, both lost, both on a journey to be found.

I met sadness by a new name in those boxes of your life. I call him regret. My grandmother's son, my mother's brother, how did we stray so far? How did we let so many seasons and so many holidays come and go?

I thought back to a moment when I was about thirteen years old coming from playing basketball. The streetlights had just come on and there you were, stumbling out of a bar. An all too familiar sight; the men in our family were always stumbling somewhere. Stumbling away from a needle, stumbling into prison, stumbling out of responsibilities. You looked at me and spoke with a drunk man's mind and hurt man's tongue: "Where are you going this time of night? Probably out fucking around just like your deadbeat father and my stupid ass brother. Ya momma raising you just like these other bitches who got pregnant too early."

I stared at you for a moment, thinking I might kill you. But I simply said, "Aight." Then walked away.

It was far from the first hurtful thing you had ever said to me, and it was far from the last, but that was the moment I was done. I relegated you to a place in which you no longer existed. A place where you would find the company of my other uncles, my father, my cousins, my grandfather, and so many other men who decided not to exist. But you were the first person that I would place there myself. I would be the patriarch of the family if no one else would.

That path ultimately broke things in me I can never fix. A Black child should always claim whatever bit of innocence they can before this country steals it.

But sitting in that 10 x 15 encapsulation of your life, I eventually found photos of all the people I thought you hated and notebooks detailing dreams you never saw come true. I found photos of my grandmother who you so often simply referred to as "a drunken bitch." But you kept her photos, so many photos. Her smiling, her laughing, her loving you. Where you couldn't find the language for your grief, you found the wrath of your anger. I know that place, too often I've called it home.

There was also an acceptance letter from the 70s to a pilot school you never had the chance to attend, but let the world tell it, you had only aspired to be an alcoholic truck driver. The world never got to know your best parts, and you only got to know the world's worst.

It was then that I realized we shared much of the same pain. Your anger and hate had been manifestations of sadness. The people who stumbled away from me stumbled away from you long before, and that's where you learned it. They, however, were gone. As imperfect as you were, you were there. You were broken. But you were there.

The addictions, violence, and trauma that forced a boy to pretend he was a man, did the same to you. We were both collateral damage of other people's internal wars.

The bottle and anger was your way to numb the pain that we are rarely given the opportunity to navigate. You were broken in the same places I was, looking for pieces of smiles and support we were never afforded. Others may not understand, but I do, I see you.

Your agony, your loneliness, our missed time—it was all by design. Generations put asunder, hoping divided we fall. Oh, how I wish someone would have caught you. That we might have spoken and shared notes from our journeys. You were trying to understand how to stop the pain, and I was trying to find what caused it. It hurts more than words can say that no one told you it wasn't your fault, told you that somewhere inside all of those people who hurt and left you, they were sorry.

My father and so many fathers like him were more victims than deadbeats. Addicts, dealers, thieves, misogynists, murderers, and corpses meant to be brothers, husbands, dads, uncles. Meant to be more, meant to be good men. They laid siege to our homes, our mothers, our fathers, and our souls. A war on Blackness that in turn made us wage a war against ourselves. This land owes you far more than you received.

We are owed our lost time, our sisters are owed respect that we've forgotten, our children are owed the dreams they've deferred. Let us have what we are owed tomorrow, and let us have what we deserve now.

I will start by telling you that you are loved, and this will not be a "goodbye," but rather a "nice to meet you."

Your nephew with all the love I have to give,
Frederick

GREEN PRISONS

cap·i·tal·ism

/ˈkapədl,izəm/

noun

~~an economic and political system in which a~~
~~country's trade and industry are controlled by private~~
~~owners for profit, rather than by the state.~~

an economic system that is inherently oppressive,
exploitative, unsustainable, and not only perpetuates
but benefits from inequality and the commodification of
marginalized people (probably you).

If you don't burn the money along with the prison
it built, they'll just use it to build another.

Capitalism knew what intersectionality was before
we did. The Black body, the white body, the woman's
body, the disabled body, the poor body, the man's body,
the trans body, all bodies and souls. Commodities at the
intersection of gain.

And then the one-legged hummingbird spiraled back
to this
reality.

Death chirps. Death chirps. Death chirps.

Screeching like nails on chalkboard while dragged from student
    to statistic.

She knows their laughter well from her father's momma's momma's
    nightmares.

Leg in hand, "where you think you're going?"

Green-eyed gluttons wonder what a leg is worth.

Cleaning freedom off glass isn't free.

Death chirps. Death chirps.

Shrieking like the brakes on her way to a dream or the same as them.

Green-eyed gluttons wonder what hummingbird feathers are worth.

As much as the sparrow? As much as the swan? As much as the
    penguin?

Death chirps.

Silenced so we can get back to work.

THE ROT IN THE GARDEN

The media taught us to wish to be someone else. The media is invested in you wanting to be another person, the same person who often wants to be another person. Because that's how the media remains interesting, and an interesting media is a wealthy media.

But nothing compares to social media. When social media was born it became the town square, a place where its creators want everyone to be. A place where lies and disagreements thrive, because lies and disagreements are more engaging than truth and agreements. Engagement keeps the town square filled, and filling the town square keeps its creators' pockets filled.

Our society is one of imagination, filled with the perpetual belief that we may all become *something*. Something bigger, better, smarter, faster, prettier, stronger. Something—more. This imagination has taken us to great heights, lifted our most marginalized, and freed many of the oppressed.

Which is why I both love and hate the media in all of its forms. It taps into and often controls this imagination and belief I'm speaking of. On their best days, television, magazines, social media platforms, etc., can help open a world of possibility and desire for us to become something different—including our best selves.

On their worst days, they're at the center of everything wrong with society, telling us that we aren't good enough, reminding us of what we don't have, and encouraging us to pull from the darkest parts of our being for likes, shares, and fame.

Every day, successful media is measured more and more by clicks and views than by morality and courage. Which is again why I despise much of the media, because it invests in people who garner attention, and that often means people doing the wrong things. More people slow down for car accidents than do for beautiful scenery.

In a world where lies spread faster than the truth and bad news sells better than good news, it seems that much of the media has invested in being its worst self—while trying to drag you and me along with it. Social media has become arguably the worst culprit, especially by feeding into toxic masculinity and misogyny.

So many of us are constantly fed this idea that our existence is somehow wrong, that we are not enough as we are. But very rarely are we asked to change in ways that might better society. Being asked to evolve emotionally, mentally, and spiritually to be better neighbors, families, and lovers is far less frequent than being asked to look and sound different. More times than not we are asked to conform to what someone else believes will make us more attractive or interesting to others. If society is a garden, it's rarely enough to be in the garden: you must have a specific scent, a specific color, have or don't have thorns.

I believe social media bolsters the idea that some flowers are worth words such as "beautiful" while others are not. The idea that only some flowers are worth time, love, appreciation, and respect is the very idea that is rotting this garden that has given us all life. The idea that only some seeds and flowers are worth sun and water is directly rooted in white supremacy, patriarchy, and capitalism. These systems thrive on the idea that it's okay for many of us to be disposable.

I believe there are two pillars upholding them, both of which need to be completely uprooted. Men and the media.

Men should be obvious, as the greatest force against women is the patriarchy and all of its tentacles, both overt and ingrained. But the media in both historic and modern senses is at the center of it all. A shadowy puppeteer, preying on and warping the imaginations and beliefs of women and men.

There is a through line from our oldest religious texts to our current social media timelines. How people should look, what constitutes a good wife, how a man should show up in the world, who has the power in relationships between the two. We are enslaved, hoping to grow in the direction of these false suns.

We must understand the impact of the media's lies, which have grown rage, hate, and narcissism in our sons, brothers, fathers, and partners. Because this force has been deeply detrimental to not only our views of women, but also our views of ourselves. But to gain this understanding, we must first understand that people have invested in us believing lies and being forced to become the most destructive forms of ourselves.

As much as some may think otherwise, there is nothing true about social media. Unlike real life, it is not made of both astounding bliss and misery. You can't curate the feeling of uncontrollable laughter with your best friend, nor can you caption the unbearable emptiness of learning that tragedy has taken them from you.

To have been elated and to have suffered is to have lived.

Most often, social media is a projection of our best selves, photos with family, vacation bathing suits, date nights with our partners. But our best selves, our best times, are only part of our stories.

What about the part where your parents are on opposite sides of the photo because they recently separated? What about the part where you returned the other bathing suit you really liked because your roommate said it made you look "fat"? What about the part where this date night is your first time seeing your partner in weeks, because that's how long it took you to forgive them for cheating?

This is not to say that the public has a right to the rest of your story but is rather an acknowledgment that there is more to it.

Perfect lives, perfect eyes, perfect smiles. These were once things to be had only by our false gods—celebrities. From Cleopatra to Beyoncé, we have fawned over and praised people we could never become. A chosen few, those who advertisers, marketers, painters, writers build monuments to. Those we could never be, their magic shrouded in mystery, and that's why we love them so.

But—what if you could be them? Better yet, what if you *should* be them?

We have just begun to have honest discussions about the impact of social media on young women and the correlation between our timelines and suicide rates, but lost in these early conversations is the impact on men and boys. If patriarchy is hell, social media is the express train there.

When I think about the role of the media in the lives of men, both traditionally and in its current iterations, I primarily consider young men. Because much of the devastation and preservation of toxic masculinity and misogyny begins very young, with boys trying to figure out who they are.

As I said before, the patriarchy feeds on many things; for me it was self-loathing. Stumbling through sorrow in my youth, I fell into the trap of toxic masculinity.

I remember girls in middle school used to say Lil' Bow Wow was cute—I had never been cute. My hair didn't look like his, my eyebrows were too thick, my clothes were too old, my acne was too bad, the gap between my teeth was too wide. Even my family wouldn't call me cute; instead, they'd say I was handsome. I knew I was too young to be handsome. It was a clever way to say they hoped I would grow into my looks. The kids at school were the only people who were honest with me.

It wasn't enough to simply be considered not cute, my classmates made sure I knew I was ugly. They had to point out my nappy hair, laugh at my thick eyebrows, let me know how old my clothes were, chop me down because my acne was bad, and shun me because the gap between my teeth was too wide.

"How dare you even be breathing on the same planet as Lil' Bow Wow?" I recall a girl in my class saying to me when she realized I had tried to get my hair braided in a style similar to that of the teen rapper she swore she would marry.

I didn't need her to tell me how disgusting I was, I already hated myself enough. Each mirror I passed reminded me how repulsive I was. Every music video shouted, "You look nothing like us." During my preteens I spent most nights crying and most days cutting school, hoping to avoid the people I thought of as truth tellers in my classes and the cafeteria.

I remember the questions I would ask myself whenever I turned on BET, MTV, NFL, NBA, or VH1. Each of these channels was filled with the boys who were cute, the boys who looked nothing like me. The boys who looked like the boys in school who used me as a prop to make the girls laugh. The girls loved it—if the girls stopped loving it, maybe the cute boys would have stopped doing it.

"Why do I have to look like this?"

"Why aren't my clothes better?"

"Why do I have to be poor?"

"Why does everybody hate me?"

"Why did God make my life like this?"

"Why does God hate me?"

"Why am I alive?"

"Why am I alive?"

"Why am I alive?"

It's a miracle that I graduated. An even greater miracle that I leaned into "this will get better" instead of "it would be better if I wasn't here." Oh, how that medicine cabinet used to call my name during those years of being treated as if I was born for classmates' amusement, as if I existed to remind the girls how much better the cute boys were.

My gym teacher saw the cute boys and the girls who liked cute boys making fun of me once. He stopped them, and when I started crying in his office, he told me to "man up." He told me he was doing me a favor. It was the last time he stopped them.

I needed to man up or I was going to die.

By the time I got to high school, cute boys didn't matter anymore. Many of the girls I wasn't cute enough for now thought they were women, because they were doing woman things, and woman things were too grown for cute boys. Woman things required men, and men were many things, but cute wasn't one of them. Luckily, during the summer heading into high school I had changed. I was tall now; working, so my clothes were new; my acne was gone; and I cut my long hair off.

To some, I had become handsome. To others, being handsome wasn't enough, a man is more than that. They needed a man. Even more than a man, at fifteen a *real* woman needed a *real* man. I wasn't a real man because I was tall but lanky, my clothes were new but didn't set trends, my acne was gone but wasn't replaced by a mustache, my hair looked better short but it wasn't cut often enough.

Real men were on BET, MTV, NFL, NBA, or VH1. They had tattoos, drove fast cars, and were showered with women. I was going to be a real man one way or another. They were going to love me. How could I make them love me?

I didn't know any real men personally, but I knew Jay-Z was a real man, Cam'ron was a real man, *Paid in Full* was about real men, Allen Iverson and Deion Sanders were real men. The kind of men whose posters were in lockers and names were doodles in notebooks of the girls who used to like the cute boys. I was going to be one of them, no matter what I had to do.

I was going to be a man. A *real* man.

I spent years clawing my way to all of the things I thought I wanted, or at least the things I thought I was supposed to want. Women, cars, popularity, respect, and admiration. But something was always missing, like I needed something, and that made me feel like less of a man.

The men I looked up to never needed anything. They were strong. They were perfect. They manned up. In spite of everything I was, I still wanted to be like them—or maybe wanted to *actually be them*.

Social media only made it worse, as now I wasn't just trying to be the men I saw on BET, MTV, NFL, NBA or VH1. I was trying to be the men I saw on Instagram, Facebook, and Twitter. The ones being the men I had always wanted to be. Always traveling, laughing, working out, taking care of the people around them, enjoying every aspect of their lives. They didn't stumble as I did. Who wouldn't want to live that perfect life? Their lives are perfect—aren't they?

I first thought about all of this when I was planning on writing this piece. It was a Wednesday, in the early hours of the morning, as the sun was still kissing the horizon. That's my favorite time to write, when everyone I love is still in bed and I don't have to worry about them. I worry a lot. My doctor thinks I should take medicine for it, but that worries me more. Those mornings bring me calm, though. When it's just me and my virus-ridden MacBook, which I should probably trade in, but I can name few more loyal.

I didn't write this piece last Wednesday morning; in fact I didn't write all day. I posted a photo on social media of my laptop to chronicle that I was about to begin writing. But instead, my morning was spent chasing our puppy, Stokely, around the apartment after being awoken by him howling at people walking by outside. I then had to walk Stokely and take him to the dog park to burn some of his energy, in the hope that this would alleviate the need to chase him throughout the day. The air was frigid that morning and the longer we stayed outside, the more my hands stiffened. He's a big dog, he needs to run a lot, meaning I was outside for a long time, and in that time my hands became so stiff they no longer felt like hands at all.

After spending most of my morning at the dog park, I brought Stokely home, where he found his favorite part of the living room rug and plopped down into slumber. I promptly sat down at my MacBook and attempted to unlock it so I could begin writing, though it was much later than I preferred and had intended. As I motioned to type my password, still stiff from what felt like arctic winds—my hands refused. This wasn't unusual to me; I had been diagnosed with multiple sclerosis nearly a decade before, and this is a typical symptom when parts of my body are met with immensely cold temperatures.

I placed my hands in the kitchen sink and ran them under hot water in hopes that this would help them loosen. It never works. But I had to try, as I wanted to write, *needed* to write. The water was unable to chisel my stone hands into tools, but it did accomplish something—it woke Stokely up. I spent the next few hours chasing him around the apartment as he ran from window to window barking at people walking by. As if he hadn't been taken to the park. As if I had been given the time to write this piece. It was now mid-afternoon.

I decided to try and pull some productivity from the jaws of this day. I headed to the home gym I'd recently created for myself on our top floor. It isn't much, but it gets the job done, and oddly enough Stokely loves watching people work out. It's one of the only things he gives you a pass to do without him barking, chewing, or howling incessantly. I changed my clothes and headed up to the gym.

There was one problem, though. I couldn't stop worrying about the fifty problems stemming from me not having written that day. As I said, I worry a lot. Sometimes those worries become anxiety, and that anxiety becomes an attack, and that attack activates parts of my multiple sclerosis—flare-ups. Making it impossible to work out, impossible to chase my puppy, impossible for anything to be possible other than sleep.

So I did.

I slept for hours, until I was awoken by the guilt of having slept for hours. The guilt of not having worked out, not having written, not having helped my fiancée chase our puppy from window to window as people walked by. I was weak, I hoped my fiancée wouldn't judge me for it. A woman like her deserved more than a weak man.

The sun had kissed the horizon again; the day was done. I lay in bed and stared at the ceiling as enough tears ran from my face to wash me into tomorrow.

Before I fully gave up on the day, I decided to go online and see what I had missed. Per usual, my timelines were filled with politics, social opinions, and inspiration. Everyone seemed to be feeling good, seemed to have accomplished so much that day. I wanted to feel good, I wanted to feel accomplished. I wiped my face, leaped out of bed, and headed upstairs to try and work out.

As I ran up the stairs Stokely heard me and promptly followed; we were both excited. I turned on some music and felt locked in, I was about to have one of my best workouts ever. Stokely walked over to where I was stretching near a mirror, so I decided to take a picture of us in the gym, ready to work. I posted the photo on Instagram, then began to attempt a pull-up. As soon as I flexed my biceps to lift my body toward the bar, I felt myself become extremely weak and tired. I was having another flare-up. My workout was done—as was my day.

I headed back downstairs and rested my defeated body back on the bed. A few minutes later I decided to read my messages on social media. One of them was in response to my photos:

"I'm not sure how you do it. But you accomplish so much every day, I need to be more like you. Way to man up," says a man whom I don't know.

A man who thinks I'm one of the men I want to be.

GASLIGHTING CULTURE

The woman said the man had murdered her brother.

The people said there should be an investigation.

The man didn't deny it, instead he complained that people were trying to cancel him.

The people supported the man. They, too, never wanted to be canceled.

I truly hope by the time you read this, the concept of "cancel culture" has fully left the collective consciousness of our society, seeing as cancel culture doesn't actually exist. Regardless of how much I may despise the concept, I feel it is important to touch upon, as it's merely an evolution of something very old and real.

Cancel culture is when people stop supporting or reject someone or a group of people based on something offensive or disrespectful they have done. Cancel culture is primarily found in online social media spaces, and the person who behaved or acted in the offensive or disrespectful way is referred to as "canceled." Some people consider this a form of ostracism.

The person or group facing said ostracism is typically a celebrity or public figure, after they have said or done something problematic or blatantly bigoted.

Most people would likely define cancel culture similarly, which makes it that much more frustrating, as there are three key points missing in my opinion. The first being the acknowledgment that the term "canceled" was appropriated from Black culture, and seemingly the film *New Jack City* (the first time I remember hearing it in the media). As is the case with most modern cultural trends, the term was popularized on Black Twitter before its co-opting. The second point is that more times than not, the people being canceled have done some form of harm and people are asking for accountability for said harm. The final point is that most people are never actually canceled.

Let's take Harry Potter author J. K. Rowling as an example. Rowling drew the ire of the queer community and their allies in the summer of 2020 for both liking a tweet that was transphobic and tweeting transphobic opinions of her own. LGBTQ+ media and the advocacy group GLAAD issued a response calling her comments "inaccurate and cruel." Many of Rowling's fans (myself included) even tried to explain to her how dangerous her views were, especially with her large platform, hoping she was simply ignorant and not bigoted.

What followed wasn't accountability from Rowling, but rather a doubling down on her opinions in a widely shared op-ed. This led to an online movement calling for her to be held accountable/canceled as well as a counter (and much larger) movement created by her fans to show their support. The movement by her fans was seemingly meant to combat the idea of canceling her, but inherently, especially with the lack of nuance on social media, it appeared to uphold and support her transphobia.

Not only was Rowling perpetuating transphobia and facing no accountability, but now there were millions of people also perpetuating transphobia in the name of combating cancel culture. As with most people facing "cancel mobs," Rowling was never in any real danger of having her career be derailed, losing financial opportunities, or being ostracized from society. All that happened was the insulation of growing ignorance and the harm to a marginalized community.

The fact of the matter is that most people lack the necessary tools and education to be held accountable for their actions. We are often taught and unconsciously socialized to act as if history doesn't matter and has no impact on current events. These are fanciful ways to lay the foundation for what actually amounts to a gaslighting culture.

At the root of cancel culture is accountability, the acknowledgment of someone's actions or views as harmful. But to negate actual accountability, people have fabricated a villainous group of people who are supposedly overcorrecting behaviors and actions. This concept, or better yet tool to circumvent accountability, has become so popularized that even the most blatantly wrong acts are now being deemed parts of cancel culture.

In spring 2021, New York governor (at the time) Andrew Cuomo was accused by more than five women, some of whom had worked for him, of sexual harassment. While I can't say whether these allegations are true, I can speak to his immediate response to them. As one would expect, he claimed the allegations were false, but he didn't stop there. He also claimed that this was just another example of cancel culture. Uhhh, no, sir, you are being accused of abusing your power and privilege to harass women, potentially hindering their careers and lives.

Even Donald Trump has said he is being "canceled" after his many bigoted statements about women, Black people, disabled people, and so many more. All while asking his base to stop supporting specific businesses and individuals, which sounds like cancellation to me. I suppose it only works one way.

As I said, most of society doesn't do well with accountability. Which is why cancel culture is such a popular talking point for powerful, or situationally powerful, people. We are on the precipice of a global reckoning about racism, sexism, ableism, classism, etc. If we continue to let this problematic talking point take up space that should be reserved for accountability and justice, we will find ourselves wasting time that could be spent dismantling oppression.

IF THESE HANDS COULD TALK

Dear Journal,

I didn't want to hurt them, I just wanted them to leave me alone. I didn't know what else to do, but it worked. They won't ever mess with me again.

I imagine most people have only been in two or three physical fights in their life. Each one of them was over something foolish. Something not worth it. They always are.

But occasionally, you find people like myself. People who have built themselves a home atop the mountain of nothingness created by violence.

As far back as we know, violence has been lauded and craved by the masses. From Achilles to Ali, we are drawn to and celebrate the most primal aspects of human nature. Big, strong, and often angry men mutilating one another. We wait in line to see films in which the stars are blood and mayhem.

But what they never tell you is that unlike the dramatization found in film and television, a fight usually lasts no more than a minute—and death takes but a second.

We romanticize and normalize, then we ask *why.*

The fracture is why. They never talk about the fracture. The way the violence splits you in half and you're never truly the same after.

I know the fracture. I've lived it, felt it, given it, been broken by it.

We don't talk about the fracture.

I pulled up on one of them dudes who jumped me the other night. Found him slippin' coming out of a restaurant with his girl. Knocked him out in three hits—you know how I do.

By the time I was thirty, I'd been in at least forty physical fights—and I cried after nearly every single one of them.

My tears had nothing to do with the outcome of the fights. To my credit, I've only lost two fair fights in my life. One loss was in middle school to a friend I decided to start making fun of because I thought doing that would make the popular kids stop picking on me. The other time was to a guy in college who I tried to use as a prop so I could impress some young women.

In both instances, I rightfully got my ass beat.

I don't believe it's coincidence that the only two fights I've ever started also happen to be the only two fights I've lost. Looking back, I'm happy I got my ass kicked. You'd be surprised how many life lessons can be found while being punched in the face.

Though I do wish I would have needed to learn only once.

The rest of my fights have found me on the right side of history—and fists. In each one I was either defending myself or standing up for someone else. As with most millennials, one of my most important fights happened at a music festival when I was in my twenties. That was when I started to realize I had a problem.

Yeah, I fought him—he shouldn't have looked at me like that.

I was waiting in a concession line when I saw a white guy spit on a young Black woman who was working at the festival. She had refused to sell him another drink because he was already extremely drunk and belligerent. So he felt entitled to spit on her.

The moment the spit made contact with her face she began lunging at him, but was held back by her coworkers. As she tried to pry herself free, the man laughed about what he had done and balled his fists, daring her to attack him.

Watching what was happening, I decided to intervene, to act as the young woman's proxy in the fight. Not only was I happy to defend a Black woman, but I thoroughly enjoyed using my fists to give white men life lessons about racism.

As soon as I stepped in front of him he swung at me. I weaved his punch and then countered with a hit so hard he probably wished his ancestors had stayed on the *Mayflower*. The fight was over as soon as it started.

Aside from his friends, everyone praised me after the fight, including the Black woman the guy had spat on. But as with every fight I'd been in, for some reason I found myself standing alone and crying uncontrollably minutes later.

When that happens, I don't feel sad or angry, it's more a feeling of being overwhelmed. As though something inside of me is trapped and trying to escape.

I wasn't going to fight him—but these niggas got eye problems.

Though I haven't been in a fight in years, I find myself in fear of whatever it is that has been trapped inside me. I know it's still there because it shows up occasionally in the way I talk to people and my defensive disposition at times. But those are things I'm working on, things I understand.

What will happen if it escapes one day and I'm unprepared?

There's a normalization and a dependence on violence in our society that I believe has trapped something in all of us, especially cisgender heterosexual men. It begins in different ways for each of us but corrodes our lives all the same. However it starts, the violence it becomes is a toxic coping mechanism for our envy, self-doubt, loneliness, and fear.

I've been chillin' lately, but how he gonna be staring at my girl like I'm not right there? What else was I supposed to do?

For Black men, violence is often used as a sword to protect ourselves within a society that has normalized systematic violence against Black men and people in general. That sword is passed down out of love to help us survive, but rarely if ever did the person giving us the weapon know how to properly wield it themselves and—more important—when not to wield it.

My mother was that person for me.

A brilliant woman, she did her best raising me as a young single parent in an impoverished neighborhood that was plagued with gangs and drugs. Like my father, hers wasn't around, and her three brothers were all too busy fighting their own demons to take part in our lives.

My mother couldn't replace those men, but she did her best to raise me as a better version of the few "good men" she knew. You know, people such as the mailman, the guy who owned the local bodega, and Carl Winslow from the show *Family Matters*.

In all seriousness, my mother gave me whatever tools she could to help me become a decent man and survive my surroundings. One of those survival tools was knowing not only how to fight, but how to win—in a place where losing could mean death.

My mother started teaching me to defend myself when I was about seven years old. She began by showing me how to make a tight fist and effectively land a punch. She would walk around me making an imaginary circle and saying, "This is your personal space, if anyone comes in it, you have a right to defend yourself." Then I'd spend the next few minutes punching her hands as if they were boxing mitts.

Though I knew how to, I was afraid to defend myself from the kids in my school and my neighborhood. I felt it was easier to let them tease me and take my toys or lunch to avoid having them beat me up.

I'm not gonna let them think I'm soft. The second they think that, it's a wrap for me. I'ma fight him as soon as I see him.

For years, I would come home with a toy missing or hungry because someone stole my lunch, and my mother would ask who did it, but I refused to tell her. So she did the only thing she could, she kept teaching me to defend myself. "If you don't make them respect you, it's going to keep happening," she'd tell me.

My mother knew that if I continued to succumb to the bullies in my school and neighborhood, at some point I would face much worse than simply having my lunch taken. The opportunity to spark that change came in the form of my first fight, which was also the day that whatever is trapped inside of me was born.

We didn't have much money when I was growing up, but my mother worked constantly to not only keep a roof over our heads, but also provide nice things for me when she could. One of those things was a surprise gift of Pokémon cards, which she had worked extra hours to afford.

I was nine years old at the time, and Pokémon was the most popular franchise in the world; it was as if there wasn't a kid on earth who didn't collect the game cards. A good collection could make or break your social standing. My mother was trying her best not only to make me happy—but also to help me fit in.

The day after my mother gave them to me, I brought my new cards to school, and for the first time, I felt like one of the popular kids. My classmates even invited me to sit with them at lunch to talk about Pokémon and video games.

I was afraid to play outside because of how the kids from my block treated me. But after the reaction at school to my new cards, I decided to bring them outside when I got home, hoping I might finally make friends.

After I got home I sat near the window and waited anxiously for the other kids to head outside. As soon as I saw them begin to play I darted out the front door to show them my cards. All of the kids were impressed. In fact, three of the older kids were so impressed, they decided to grab me and take my entire collection.

This is our neighborhood, we couldn't just let them stroll in like they ran the place. This ain't the north side, we ain't afraid of nobody over here.

Two of them held me down while the third snatched my card book out of my hands. I begged them to stop and tried explaining that my mother had worked tirelessly to buy them for me, but they didn't care. "Fuck your mother," one said as he punched me in the face and laughed.

When they walked away, I sat on the sidewalk, my ego more bruised than my body. I felt horrible about having to break the news to my mother, who had wasted both time and money she didn't have to spare.

I eventually mustered the courage to walk upstairs to our apartment and explain to my mother what had happened. When I was done, she rushed to the bathroom, grabbed a washcloth, and placed ice in it. As she went to place it on my face where I had been punched, she stopped and stared at me for a moment, then put the washcloth on a nearby table.

"Go get the cards, Freddy," she said, blank-faced with a rare seriousness.

"Huh?" I responded, completely baffled.

"Give me your house keys and don't come back until you make those boys give you the cards," she replied.

I handed her the keys, trembling with fear. "But, Mommy, I can't! They won't give them to me!"

She pushed me out the front door and slammed it in my face. "You heard what I said, boy!"

I stood outside the door for a few minutes and cried, then walked downstairs, sat in front of the building, and cried some more. Over the next few hours my time was split between walking up to our apartment door to beg my mother to let me in and watching the kids play with my cards while pointing at me and laughing.

Like I said, I had a fear of playing outside because of the kids on my block. But what I feared more than them was being outside at night without my mother. I was more than aware that the area I lived in was riddled with crime and violence during the day, and the last thing I ever wanted was to see first-hand how bad it was at night.

The instant I saw the streetlights come on, a wave of existential terror washed over me. I ran upstairs one more time and knocked on our apartment door until my knuckles were raw—no response.

When I walked back downstairs it was dark outside, but the kids who took my cards were still on the block. "Aren't their parents worried about them?" I wondered, as my mother would normally not let me be out alone that late.

I decided to walk up to the kids and ask for my cards again. "It's dark and my mom won't let me in without the cards," I told them. "Can I please have them so I can get in and then give them to you tomorrow to borrow? We can do that every day."

It seemed like a good plan at the time. I would keep my life, and they could show off with the cards again the next day.

All of us are gonna miss a few games because of suspension; Coach said we let our teammates down. But it was worth it. Couldn't just let them rich white boys stroll onto our field like they run the place.

"Fuck you and your mom, she's a bitch," one of the kids responded to my offer.

"Don't call my mom that!" I said through clenched teeth while balling my fists.

"He ain't gon' do nothing! Your mother a bitch!" another kid said.

I stood there for a moment that seemed to last for eternity. I was angrier than I had ever been in my life. I didn't care about the Pokémon cards anymore or getting back into the apartment; respect was the only thing on my mind. They didn't have to respect me, but they were going to respect my mother.

I walked up to the first kid, who called my mother a bitch, and punched him in his stomach. The hit knocked the air out of him, forcing him to hunch over in pain, which gave me the opportunity to punch him in the face. He immediately dropped to the ground. The other two kids stared at me, stunned, until they both began swinging at me.

I'm not allowed in the club anymore, we got kicked out for a brawl. We fought these niggas came in trying to stunt. Buying bottles trying to be all up in my homie's girl's face, strolling around like they ran the place.

I backpedaled away to dodge the kids' punches as my mother had taught me, then picked up a large piece of broken wood to defend myself. One of the kids came darting toward me, so I swung the wood at him as hard as I could and hit him directly on the side of his face, making him fall.

Then the first kid I hit began to get up, so I hit him in the back with the piece of wood to knock him down again.

The third kid began to run away with my book of Pokémon cards, so I chased him down and jumped on his back to stop him. My added weight forced him to the ground, at which point I began to punch him as he attempted to cover his face. I kept punching until I noticed the blood on my fists from his nose. I stood there in shock, looking back and forth from the three kids to my bloody knuckles.

I couldn't believe what had happened—what I had done.

Something died in me that moment. Maybe it was innocence, maybe it was fear, I'm still not sure. Either way, what happened next led me down the path of who I became for the next twenty years.

It was as if I had blacked out, and when I came to I realized that some of the adults and other kids from the block were egging me on and saying things such as "Okay, Tyson!" I didn't know what to do. I saw my book of cards lying on the ground right next to a book that belonged to one of the three kids. I took both and ran home.

When I arrived upstairs my mother was waiting in the doorway. "Are you okay?"

"Yeah. I got my cards back," I responded.

"I know. But are you okay?" she replied in a worried and guilty tone.

"I'm fine," I replied coldly, not knowing that I was far from it.

We were both drunk, he was talkin' mad shit, and we got into an argument over the game. Thankfully my boys got me out the bar before the cops came.

I walked to my room and lay in bed silent the rest of the night, thinking about how I hurt those kids, confused about why it felt so good. I wanted more; there was still something I needed to get out, still other kids standing around who had made fun of me before. Kids who deserved to be beat, too.

I grew so frustrated that I hadn't hurt them as well that I began to cry in frustration until I cried myself to sleep.

After that day, none of the kids on my block bothered me; word had gotten around about how bad I had hurt the older kids. In fact, I had broken one of their noses from what one parent told my mother. I couldn't tell whether she was disappointed or proud. Either way, I didn't get in trouble.

From my perspective, people finally stopped bullying me when I showed that I could defend myself. I needed the kids at school to know, too, so the next time someone bothered me there, I was happy to oblige their disrespect with my fist.

But no matter how many people I fought, there was always someone new who tested me, someone else who tried to hurt me. Fighting became my new normal, violence for the sake of my freedom and respect, like Maximus in *Gladiator*—"Are you not entertained?"

It was never enough, I was never freed.

He saw me holding her hand, I couldn't let him disrespect me in front of her. Couldn't let her think I'm soft.

Years later, I learned that my mother had been watching everything unfold from her bedroom window. She wanted to make sure I was okay, but couldn't step in. The reason she sent me outside to get the cards was because she was worried that if she didn't force me to become "tougher" she would lose me to the neighborhood because I was too "soft," or eventually to a white supremacist world because I was a Black boy who was too "weak."

My mother's lesson most likely saved my life, and for that I'm forever grateful. If you remain a sheep, the wolves will eventually eat you. But if you turn someone into a wolf, you should also make sure that it doesn't simply follow the rest of the pack.

She did what she felt "a father or an uncle would have done." She did what the patriarchy has conditioned us to do. But there is something other than the sheep and the wolf, there is the bird. The bird learns to fly, the bird is free.

Those three kids weren't much different from me. We were all dealing with the trauma of being poor and Black in America. We may all have been fatherless, we may all have been bullied, we may all have been in pain. Instead of finding community, we found violence.

If I look past my fear and anger, I can see the glow of the streetlights on their faces as they smiled at each other. There is a miracle to be found in every smile of a Black child. I wish I could go back and talk to all of us, I wish I could tell all of us that we have wings.

I heard her telling her friends that I'm sensitive—I think she was gonna leave me because she thought I was soft. So, I fought that one dude from around the *corner in front of her. You know, the one who was talking all that shit at the courts a few weeks ago. Yeah, ol' what's-his-name's friend.*

So many of us are harboring trauma from the time we are born, fueled by it, molded by it. Many of our violent actions are simply the manifestations of something deeper, something unspoken.

I wasn't fighting the kids who stole my Pokémon cards, I was fighting the ghosts of all the men who never wanted to be in my life. The same way I wasn't only hitting the white man who spat on the young Black woman, I was hitting all the white men who I've seen disrespect or harm Black people with no repercussions.

In my heart, those people were the embodiments of everything and everyone who had hurt me. But in reality, I was never even fighting them, I was fighting myself. That's why I cried after every fight—because even when I won, I lost.

What *actually* hurts?

As much as we want them to, the black eyes and bloody knuckles will never heal the poverty, the anxiety, the obstacles, the expectations, the pain.

We were taught to survive, and that violence is the way to do it. Violence is a tool, and like any tool, it's useful in some instances, but not all.

I just got me a little gun, too. People ain't fighting fair no more—but they gonna know I'm not the one. Not afraid. Not soft.

You can break open a door with a hammer, but you are meant to use a key. If all you have is your fist, everything looks like something to punch.

Violence perpetrated by cisgender heterosexual men is an especially deadly epidemic, but as with any virus, you can't eradicate something unless you know where it started. As individuals and a community, cisgender heterosexual men need to identify *how* we are violent, as there are physical, verbal, and mental manifestations. This is the work of protecting those around us.

Then we need to look at the root of *why* we are violent. This is the work of healing ourselves. Working on the why is the most difficult fight you'll ever have. But once you do that, you'll hold weapons that will truly help you win—maybe even help you rest.

I'm tired of losing the fight.

I just came from my bro's funeral. Somebody shot him—the guy said he "looked at him disrespectfully."

IMPACT
OR
(THE UNBELIEVABLE
PAIN CAUSED)

THE BLOOD OF FORTY-FOUR

Dominique "Rem'mie" Fells

Riah Milton

Monika Diamond

Yampi Méndez Arocho

Neulisa Luciano Ruiz

Dustin Parker

Lexi

Scott/Scottlynn DeVore

Johanna Metzger

Serena Angelique Velázquez Ramos

Layla Pelaez Sánchez

Penélope Díaz Ramírez

Nina Pop

Helle Jae O'Regan

Tony McDade

Jayne Thompson

Selena Reyes-Hernandez

Brayla Stone

Merci Mack

Shakie Peters

Bree Black

Summer Taylor

Marilyn Monroe Cazares

Brian "Egypt" Powers

Dior H Ova (aka Tiffany Harris)

Queasha D Hardy

Aja Raquell Rhone-Spears

Kee Sam

Lea Rayshon Daye

Aerrion Burnett

Mia Green

Michelle Michellyn Ramos Vargas

Felycya Harris

Brooklyn DeShauna Smith

Sara Blackwood

Angel Haynes

Yunieski Carey Herrera

Asia Jynaé Foster

Chae'Meshia Simms

Skylar Heath

Kimberly Fial

Jaheim Pugh Jaheim Barbie

Courtney "Eshay" Key

Alexandria Winchester

And they stepped onto the tallest thing they could find and yelled, "Because I am!"

This essay was written in 2020, prior to Dave Chappelle's 2021 Netflix special The Closer, *in which many claimed that he was doubling down on his transphobic views.*

Two things happened during 2020, which, on the surface, may seem completely siloed from one another but in reality are intrinsically linked.

Dave Chappelle won a Grammy and an Emmy award for his Netflix stand-up comedy special *Sticks & Stones*, and by the end of the year there were forty-four known murders of transgender and gender-nonconforming people in America. The highest number on record within a calendar year.

If you haven't heard about these murders before, don't be surprised. A quick Google search reveals that most media outlets didn't cover them, as is often the case with the strategic erasure of lives existing beyond more mainstream binaries. Well, of course, unless they are punch lines in one of Dave Chappelle's many anti-trans jokes. Which are ever so lauded by right-wing nationalist outlets such as Breitbart, who said, "Dave Chappelle just might save America" in response to Chappelle's rancid transphobia (among other issues) in his award-winning stand-up special.

Let me start by saying, I don't believe Chappelle's jokes are the sole cause of the murder of forty-four transgender people, but I do think that he is a symbol of an epidemic for which cisgender men and women are to blame. The people pulling the threads that are unraveling the entire ball of yarn.

Growing up I was a huge fan of Dave Chappelle, like the type of fan who can still rehash many of his skits from *Chappelle's Show* word for word. I'd go as far as saying he was a hero of mine. I idolized what felt like an unapologetic Blackness and self-assuredness that I was in search of within myself. Chappelle had a way of very loudly and directly saying the often unsaid things in the minds and hearts of those who may have felt voiceless. This was best represented and appreciated when he was punching up at white supremacy and the wealth class in a way that was both hilarious and deeply revealing.

Chappelle had a finger on the pulse of the ugliest parts of society, which he used comedy to turn a mirror upon. Not only for laughter but seemingly for thoughtful analysis, reflection, and potential change. I would argue that all great artists are also sociologists and historians, and Chappelle always seemed a bit of both. Someone who can conceptualize what is happening around them and give context to it in a way that is relatable and illuminating. This was on full display during Chappelle's Netflix special *8:46*, in which he publicly ruminates on the murder of George Floyd and the systems designed to justify his public lynching. As has been the case since Chapelle's earliest days of comedy, it is obvious he constantly considers the plight of the Black man in America. But based on his constant anti-trans and other incendiary misogynist jokes, it's become more obvious that he doesn't consider much more than that.

Chappelle, like all of us, exists at the intersection of various oppressions. Yet he fails to understand that he also lives at the intersection of many privileges (more so now), and in turn, his comedy is often more a shield for our demons than for our angels.

In other words, where he was once looking up at ivory towers and using his talents to tear them down, he is now looking down from those same ivory towers and using his talents to tear down the people looking up at him.

This is not to say that the Chappelle of my youth was without flaws. His comedy has always been riddled with homophobia, misogyny, and anti-Blackness. Which in many ways is sadly a reflection not just of him, but of the times we lived in. Though this is not an excuse, it is the truth. Much of the culture and language for inclusion and intersectionality is new to many people.

The word "bitch" was more normalized in music that I listened to as a young person than the air I breathed, as was the token Black woman from the hood with multiple "baby daddies" on television, and the ever-bubbly gay man who was the constant target of pedophilia jokes in film. It was, and still is, a deeply problematic time, one that people such as my uncles, aunts, and Chappelle are still stuck in. In many ways he is the embodiment of a problem that is much bigger than he is. Which is why his more recent comedy has been so deeply disappointing and, more important, dangerous.

In *Sticks & Stones* Chappelle spends much of his time making dated, problematic jokes about sexual abuse, cancel culture, and the trans community. This comes after having received a great deal of criticism about doing much the same during his 2017 Netflix special, *Equanimity*. He begins *Sticks & Stones* by speaking to his understanding of some of his critics' points, with acknowledgments such as "I'm what's known on the streets as a victim-blamer." He later laments the constant calls for accountability that celebrities face from said victims: "I'm sorry, ladies, I've got a fucking #MeToo headache."

Many people were angry with Chappelle after *Sticks & Stones*, saying he "doubled down" on his oppressive jokes even after being criticized for them before. But I disagree with that analysis. Though these jokes are still appalling, there is an obvious change in tone and delivery between his jokes in *Equanimity* and the ones in *Sticks & Stones*, which may have something to do with a fellow comedian and fan of his named Daphne Dorman. Daphne happened to be a transgender woman.

Chapelle spoke about Daphne during *Sticks & Stones*, saying that they had become friends and that she was "laughing the hardest" at his jokes, seemingly including the anti-trans ones. He tokenized her to absolve himself of the critiques that he was being transphobic. It was his way of telling audiences and critics that he understands some of the outrage and potential ramifications of what he is doing. It's not lost on him that for my cousins, my uncles, his growing base of Trump-supporting fans, hearing these anti-trans jokes may ignite and reaffirm their ugliest parts—he just doesn't care. Unless it's the life of a Black man, a life that could have been his, it's a punch line.

Daphne Dorman died by suicide just weeks after the premiere of *Sticks & Stones*. I can't say why she made the decision to take her own life, but I can present the fact that over 40 percent of transgender adults say they've attempted suicide in their lifetime. Citing social and cultural discrimination, mental abuse, physical violence, and constant harassment. Chappelle's "jokes" are written in blood.

But this isn't just about Dave Chappelle, this is about those of us whose lives depend on truth being spoken to power but are unable to see when we are the powerful ones. People like you, like me, like our uncles, aunts, friends, and family. Those who would claim they fight for Black lives while ignoring the fact that the life span of a Black trans woman is just thirty-five years.

This is about the normalization of forty-four trans lives being taken for simply having the audacity to be more than our jokes, more than our punch lines, and more than our slurs. This isn't about canceling each other but rather about asking each other to evolve. This also isn't solely about Dave Chappelle; he is merely a symptom of something much larger than himself. Though people like him make it more difficult to cure the ailment. This is about becoming creatures of freedom for our own sake and understanding that sticks and stones may not break bones, but your words are the influence. Your words are the justification.

OF MONSTERS AND MEN

She trusted Bill because he raised a generation. He named her liar as if he was there when she was born, so his children called her by that name. His children liked this name, it made them feel good about themselves. So, they began changing other women's names to liar as well.

The details of the moon enlighten, face me, devil—
Agony is his name.
And we praise you, father
And we dream of you, uncle
And we hope for you, brother
Secret door in this Black ivory tower, there is no laughter here—
Sixty times I ask my father what he is doing.
But whistlin' lies and cotton-gin fans
But never is what justice serves
But what about the poplar trees?
This, I know . . .
Southern breeze.
This, I know . . .
Blood at the root.

Ransacked hopes and looted bodies, the wounds bare it all—
Mirage as your sword.
Reveal the wolf of the herd
Reveal one who would batter his rib
Reveal a reason to leave weed for serpents
Tears of your youth flood grayer years' dungeons, you are known
     to us now—
I must find my own name, William.
The shields will not be the keloids on your backs
The shelters will not be the levels of the inferno
The lies will not be the flesh I call my own
This mirror offers more than your father.

THE HYPOCRISY OF HOTEPS AND THE BOURGEOISIE

She had two blind dates that weekend, both with guys who her friends set her up with.

The first date was on a Saturday night; her friend told her that he was just her type. "I met him at a party he invited a friend of mine to. His place is amazing! He went to an HBCU for undergrad and an Ivy League school for grad school, just like you. He's always in a tailored suit because he works in finance. You're going to love him!"

So, she went on the date, which she hated every minute of. After the date she called her friend to tell her why she didn't enjoy herself.

"What do you mean he doesn't care about Black people living in poverty? Proximity to whiteness? What are you talking about? What does showing up in a suit on a Saturday night have to do with Black boys being murdered by police? Respectability politics? What are you talking about?"

The second date was the next afternoon; her other friend told her that he was just her type. "I met him at the Roots Picnic last summer with his friends. He was real cool. Never hit on me or anything like that, called me "queen" the entire time. He's into all the things you're into, Erykah Badu, incense, sage, Malcolm, Angela, all that Blackity Black stuff. You're going to love him!"

So, she went on the date, which she hated every minute of. After the date she called her friend to tell her why she didn't enjoy herself.

"What do you mean he told you going to brunch was 'white'? He said what about you also liking music by white artists? He called Black people at Ivy leagues 'sellouts'? What do you mean he refused to let the waiter serve him because he was a Black gay man?"

I considered not writing this piece because it's such a nuanced conversation that requires a great deal of learning and unlearning to truly be had. But I'm hoping people will make considerations and seek out knowledge. I'd suggest watching the 2021 documentary *Exterminate All the Brutes* by brilliant director Raoul Peck. He does a marvelous job of unraveling the strings that have pulled, orchestrated, and bound the Western world and its people.

That said, the first point I'll make is that Blackness is not a monolith. As with people belonging to any group, there are varied interests, beliefs, and experiences amongst Black people globally. While that is also true of the Black Americans who descend from ancestors plagued by the oppression of chattel slavery, there is a commonality in how we have been shaped. Sadly, also in how we've been molded.

Though the prevailing mainstream narrative has been that America was founded on ideas and principles of freedom and liberation, the reality is that the reason the country exists is in direct opposition to both. The land America occupies was first colonized with the sole intent of expanding the capitalistic endeavors of white Europeans, and more times than not, white Europeans who were men. Meaning that the country was actually founded upon three ideas and principles: capitalism, white supremacy, and patriarchy.

The brutality and extermination faced by the Native Americans who lived on North American soil for centuries was all in the name of these ideas. The blood-soaked fields and the soul-stealing shackles that bound stolen Black beings were in the name of these principles. The fact that these atrocities weren't committed purely in the name of hatred makes them feel more sickening to me. Because it shows just how easily people or actions become commodities and "necessary evils" within a society driven by capitalism, patriarchy, and white supremacy.

Because the Black American experience is not monolithic, and the influence of these ideas and principles exists on a spectrum, there are those of us who don't see how we are actually upholding the very ideas and principles that have ravaged the Black American community. There are also those who are fully cognizant and don't care for various reasons, such as those benefiting from consciously and strategically helping uphold these influences. But that's a different conversation entirely, and the focus right now is on groups who don't necessarily realize they are upholding these influences. Popular culture often refers to these groups as "hoteps" and "the Black bourgeoisie." So for the sake of this conversation, I'll use those titles.

A hotep is often defined as a Black person who considers themselves to be pro-Black and knowledgeable about how institutions of whiteness have oppressed Black people. This group often leans heavily into afro-centric attire and what could be considered afro-centric aesthetics and vernacular. All this is conceptually great on the surface; even I would have considered myself a hotep if that was all there was to it.

"The Black bourgeoisie" is often used as a name for Black people living in the economic upper or upper-middle class of America. As is the case in most class structures, being members of these classes more times than not is directly correlated to access and privilege within various other systems, such as education. Again, conceptually great on the surface; why wouldn't we want more Black people escaping a life of poverty?

The issue is that people in both groups often fail to see how they themselves are not only upholding the systems they are trying to be liberated from, but are also plunging other Black people further into them.

Hoteps' failure is often rooted in misogyny, homophobia, and transphobia. Many men and women who would be deemed hoteps have an acute lens as it relates to the liberation of cis-gender Black men, and how the judicial, educational, class, and media systems have oppressed those Black men. But their lens often doesn't extend much further. They fail to see that the systems they rail against are designed not solely against Black men, but rather against Black people as a whole. Cisgender Black men can't be liberated unless all Black people are liberated. If anyone is still suffering under the rule of these systems, the systems aren't destroyed or dismantled. These systems don't care about the designations of identity, they care about Blackness.

It's a strategically designed feature of the oppressive systems hoteps combat that makes them believe they are the sole victims of oppression while at the same time victimizing and oppressing other Black people.

American principles and ideas have conditioned Black people to gatekeep; to decide who is and isn't worthy of being liberated is a distraction from any true liberation.

The failures of the Black bourgeoisie can be compared to those of hoteps as they relate to unconsciously upholding Black oppression in America, but they are not mirrors. Oftentimes without their realizing it, the failures of the Black bourgeoisie lie in their belief that liberation can come from climbing the ranks to gain access and power within structures and institutions oppressing Black people. This is the false narrative that far too many Black people are conditioned to believe: that representation, respectability, and financial freedom can somehow save Black people from America's ideas and principles. Barack Obama becoming the first Black president did not stop a white supremacist from becoming president immediately after. A Black man in a suit is no more protected from a white supremacist's bullet than a Black man in a hoodie, and having the money to drive a luxury vehicle rather than sit on a bus doesn't lessen a Black person's chances of being murdered by police.

The issue isn't access and power, the issue is the existence of the system itself. More Black people becoming police officers doesn't stop Black people from being murdered by police. The only difference with more Black police would be that Black people may be murdered by someone who looks like them.

A Black person who has money or education within white supremacist, capitalist, and patriarchal structures isn't indicative of systemic change. While there are more Black American billionaires than ever in this country's history, the racial wealth gap is also the largest it has been in over a century. An individual's "Black excellence" is a manifestation of Black exceptionalism and does not lift any other Black people out of the struggles they were born in. Thus it doesn't truly lift someone in the Black bourgeoisie out of their struggles either; like the hoteps they can be reclaimed by the systems at any point. If the systems still exist, a Black family living in a new house can quickly become the Black family in the street.

EXPECTATIONS AND SHADOWS

Before she left her house that morning she looked in the mirror and said, "I am worthy because I am enough." Later, she rushed to find ten mirrors during the day, which was better than eleven the day before.

On the tenth time she found a mirror in a restroom at the train station on her way home. Breathing heavily, she darted through the door of the restroom and placed her phone down on the sink. Then she looked in the mirror and said, "I am worthy because I am enough."

A few minutes later she exited the restroom and walked to her train to head home. When she got on the train she saw one of her coworkers—she gave him a slight smile. He responded by anxiously putting his head down as if he hadn't seen her. She put her head down and closed her eyes as she held on to the rail. "I am worthy because I am enough."

The man walked off the train at the next stop. As he did, he looked back to see if she was watching, but her head was still down. As the train left with her on it, the man sighed deeply. "All you had to do was say hello." He sighed again and said to himself, "I am worthy because I am enough."

[A warm spring night in 2006, on a parkway driving back to the south side of Yonkers.]

These drives home by myself always give me a chance to think. Something I don't get to do much of because I'm always too busy going. Going—nowhere. (Don't do that, you have plans.) I'm always playing the role I was given, a role I knew before knowing anything else. Before my favorite song. Before crying during rom-coms. Before my favorite ice cream. Before I knew who I was, as if I've ever had a chance to figure that out.

So much time spent thinking about how to fill shoes that other people didn't want to wear. "Don't worry, Mom; don't worry, Grandmommy; don't worry, Cousin; don't worry, Cousin's Son. I'm still here."

But when I do think about something else, I think about sometimes feeling like the only place I'm going is to the grave. But driving at night, listening to Thelonious and Trane—this is when I'm free. I don't even call it a car when I'm in it, I call it a chance. I can go anywhere if I really want to, and I would, I swear I would. But I can't. They need me, to be here, to be there, to be more. But the second I get my mother and grandmother out the south side I don't know where I'm going to go, but I'm gone. I'm going to put them in a house, probably somewhere in Connecticut, where all the white folks live. A place with a big garden, Grandmommy would love that. She always wanted to grow things, but you can't grow anything in the projects except anger and sadness.

There would be a big room for hosting parties with a nice homemade bar like the ones on HGTV. I love those shows, but I only watch them when I'm by myself now, ever since she saw me watching them and laughed, saying it was "soft." But when I do get to watch them, I think about my mother's friends coming over and not having to worry about leaving early in case niggas are shooting that night, or having to go make sure their car radio is still there. Everyone on the block is going to talk about me and smile because I got my family out, just like Juan from around the corner did. But I'm not like Juan, I'm not going to stay around like he did. He should have left the neighborhood and the game when he had a chance. I wish more people realized being greedy and being desperate are cousins. A lot of dudes don't have other plans; you can't hustle forever. Your mom doesn't need a Benz, she needs a way out.

It's like Don Corleone said in *The Godfather,* "I spent my whole life trying not to be careless. Women and children can afford to be careless, but not men." One of the earliest things I learned was that a man's job is to have a plan to provide for his family and not be reckless. I'm smarter than Juan and them, I'm going to put in work until I graduate and then we're all gone.

Maybe I'll get into USC, even though Ms. Henderson said it was a long shot. "Even if you somehow get accepted, how would you pay for it? Someone like you is going to need a full ride, and I doubt you'll get one. You should think more about community college; it's a step up from where you're at now and far less expensive." I try not to think about the things she says. She didn't tell the other honors students to think about community college. The only reason I was still going to the guidance counselor's office anyway was because they had the college application fee waivers. But since I can't have any more of those, I can just figure it out on my own—like everything else. I have the grades to get in and get a scholarship. If I keep stacking this money I won't even need a full ride.

Imagine me lying on a beach in California! I haven't been to a beach since I was kid, no time for it, and we didn't have a car to get there until I got this hooptie. I think kids should be near water as often as possible, because water feels like possibility. When I get to California I'm going to go to the beach all the time; I'll even go to a few Lakers games! I've never had enough money to go to an NBA game before, and I haven't seen Kobe play since he was in high school, when my cousins from Philly took me. Man, I knew he was going to be great from the moment he stepped on the court. He went off that night, dropped like forty, and then after there were people from the news everywhere. He was so calm, like it was nothing, like the world didn't get to tell him who he was, and they respected him for it. I've never seen somebody young and Black respected like that.

He still gets that respect, even after that case a few years back. I remember the old heads in the shop wouldn't even allow there to be a conversation about whether he did it or not. "Kobe ain't do that shit! I know blackmail when I see it. They always do this to ours. Now, I'm not saying Kobe didn't cheat. Ain't nothing wrong with a little cheating here and there, but what would Kobe want her for? Kobe could have anybody. Hell, look how bad his wife is. Shit, if Kobe don't know what to do with it—I know what to do with it!"

They were always carrying on like that. I didn't always agree with them, but I knew my place. The old heads in the shop basically raised the neighborhood. It felt good to have older men to be around who knew so much more than I did, even if it was only for a few hours a week to get a cut. When people talked about Kobe they never mentioned how smart he was, speaking all of those languages and whatnot. I loved watching him in interviews after the game, he would speak Spanish and Italian with some of the journalists. I had never seen anything like it, he could do anything. I read that he grew up in Italy. Besides the Jamaicans and Ghanians around the way, I don't think I've ever met a Black person who grew up in another country. Matter of fact, outside of Jamaica and Ghana, I don't think I know any Black people who've even left this one.

[The wind picks up in the car.]

(Pick your papers up off that seat before they fly out the window. Have some sense.) I really can't believe I still have to do all of this homework when I get in. Maybe I should start letting one of the girls in my class do my homework when the season starts, like Coach Matthews suggested. It would definitely help, especially on nights like this, when my last guests refused to leave the restaurant so I could go home. It's *Red Lobster*, not a damn nightclub. It must be at least twelve in the morning. If I didn't have to keep this job for appearances I would never go back. It's not that I mind working a regular gig, but people on the block were right, I make more in an hour hustling than in an entire night pushing crab legs. On top of that, what woman is going to respect a man who smells like fish and biscuits all the time? At least that's what she told me. (You were the problem.) Before I left I would tell my manager that he's wrong. Wrong about the cooks, wrong about the busboys, wrong about all the people he hires for less because he knows they can't get a job anywhere else. Wrong like every other white man I had met in my life was about me.

[Sirens in the distance.]

(Focus. Get home.) I know I should be home already, but those rich white girls at Sarah Lawrence are my best customers and on nights when people aren't tipping, I can't afford to not answer their call. There were a lot of white girls at my school but most of them weren't like this, these are the types of white girls who grew up with everything. The only thing these types of white girls ever seem to want is to feel something. It's like they do everything in their power to get closer to death so they can feel more alive. I wish I could just take it from them. Everything they're taking for granted. I don't even need a lot of it, I just want something. Most of the time, it doesn't even feel as if we live in the same world. Every time I stop by their school it gives them a chance to let me know what life is like on their planet.

They think they're so deep, think they're profound. "My mother called me again, she's so annoying. I don't care about who just moved into the house down the block from us in Greenwich, Connecticut! People are dealing with real things in other places! She just doesn't get it." They say things like this to each other constantly, even louder when they can tell I'm listening. As they hand me the cash they say things like "I'm sure your mom is so much cooler than my mom. My mom's never been through anything." My mom had been through more than anything, she had been through everything there was to go through from what I could tell. But I never told these white girls that; I never told them anything about me or my life. They always compare themselves to us. Praising us for our "perseverance" and how we overcome obstacles they assume we faced. I know why I'm obsessed with thinking about them—because they have everything and can take the little that's mine whenever they want. But I can never understand why they are so obsessed with us. Besides my name, they've never really asked anything, and they can barely even remember that. They're always too busy assuming.

"What about Black people? You don't do anything for them! You just don't get it!" I'm sure they tell their parents as they think of me or some other Black person they think they're close to but won't offer a seat or glass of water when that person is stopping by. I'm sure they decided to go to Sarah Lawrence because it was in *The Notebook*. They bring up the fact that their school was in the film almost as often as they do their resentment for their parents. Each time telling me about what makes Ryan Gosling so special, as if I care, or as if I haven't already said I've seen the film numerous times. They erase me in real time as I tell them I exist. They don't listen, not to me anyway. They just want to talk over people who can't talk over them—like the mothers they resent. But they have money, and that's something that makes this all worth it. (You haven't listened to "C.R.E.A.M." in a while.) There are so many things I would rather be doing, but these college applications aren't going to pay for themselves, the lights aren't going to stay on by themselves, my mother shouldn't have to do it all herself, my grandmother shouldn't have to do it all herself.

(Don't forget if you can't get her those Jordans and that matching jacket that her friend in class had, then she might as well be by herself. You'd hate for her to cheat on you like she did.) I don't want that, don't want her to find someone who will take care of her because I can't. Her heart is good, and she deserves the things she wants that the tv tells her she should. All the things her father told her she didn't deserve, because he couldn't afford to buy them for her. He lost his job months ago when the sugar plant closed and hasn't paid rent in months. He was there for fifteen years before that, ever since she was born. He was in the army before that and got hurt. He had no skills when he came home, so the sugar plant saved his life. But all the factories and plants were gone, and the only other skill he had was finishing beer cans.

When he wasn't in the street feeling bad for himself, he was in the apartment they were about to lose telling her and her mother they weren't shit. At one point, he called her mother "fat bitch" so much that she had to remind her mother that wasn't her name. Then her mother started taking her grief and laying it at her daughter's feet: "Don't you think you're getting a bit fat?" Now for the last few weeks, all she eats is celery. At night her father will randomly stop by the living room that doubles as her bedroom as she's studying for exams to tell her she's too stupid to pass. The same exams will make her mother say, "You think you're better than me?" if she finds out how good a student she is. She's starting to ask me if she's stupid, and getting annoyed with me for not telling her "she looks fat." Neither are true. Too skinny. Too big. Too smart. Too dumb. Too loud. Too quiet. The lies so many of the girls I know believe about themselves. Lies that become a woman's truth. I don't know how to make her happy again, but my mother said a man who cares about you will provide, so that's what I'll do.

God bless the child that's got his own—so he can give it to others.

[Another. Siren. Wailing. Closer.]

(Lord, please don't let the cops stop me.) Jazz is the only thing that keeps me calm when I'm driving from a sale in these white areas. I don't have anything on me, but I know just as well as the cops do that Black people don't be in this area—let alone a seventeen-year-old Black kid with cocaine under my seat. They'll think I'm either coming from stealing something or sleeping with a white girl, and who knows what they'll do to me if they assume I was sleeping with a white girl. Like the police, the news would call me a grown man to justify it. They did that to Kenny. We used to play basketball together. He had a white girlfriend in Ardsley. Her father was on the police force and caught them in bed. She thought he would be busy in the Black neighborhoods harassing other niggas who looked like Kenny that night.

But not that night. Even though Kenny jumped out the window, her father recognized him, and found him a few weeks later. Kenny's funeral was a closed casket, word around was that when his body turned up you could barely recognize him. News said it was gang violence, but Kenny wasn't ever in any gangs, always with his white girl or working on his game. I don't know what happened to her, she might go to Sarah Lawrence. (Don't cry. Kenny would want you to get home.)

I don't want to think about cops anymore, it makes me angry, sad, makes me nervous. Makes me think about that Rodney King video my mother showed me back in the day. "This is why we can't call the police if something happens to us. They're out to get you." (You think Kenny got that advice?) Shit, even the security guards at Sarah Lawrence looked at me like they wished they were cops, wished they could do more than just ask who I knew there and what the nature of my visit was. (Put in a CD. It will help clear your mind. Maybe your oldies.) "Betcha by Golly Wow" by the Stylistics is always my jam, and I'm acting surprised like I'm not the one who made the playlist. "Oooo, this is it right here!" I sound like the old heads at the barbershop, and my third cousins from Philly who I hadn't seen since I was younger because life happens. The third cousins I wished were my first cousins or my uncles, the ones I wished were around more to help play some of these roles.

I always say music was better back then, even though I wasn't alive whenever back then was. My grandmother says I'm an old soul. That's what they tell the children who had to learn to be adults before they ever had the chance to be children. She would be heartbroken if she knew I was out here doing this, but where else would I be that would allow me to secretly leave those twenties in her coat pockets that she keeps finding? I'm mad it's only twenties, twenties won't get her out of the projects. I'm mad she had three sons, and three other grandsons, and I'm the only one trying to get her that house with the garden she gave up on dreaming about. She says that when I was born she told everyone in the family I was going to be the person who saves us. She had four children and seven grandchildren at the time, so that couldn't have made them feel good. Either way, I'm trying to live up to it. But there was so much to save us from. (Why do I have to be out here worrying about the police when all the other men in the family are somewhere worrying about themselves?)

Grandmommy saw something in me she didn't see in the rest of the family anymore, not because she didn't want to, but because they had turned off all the lights. She had lost her first husband, though she didn't tell me how he died, but I knew he was a "good man." Hardworking, backbreaking, non-complaining, a provider. I had spent all seventeen of my years trying to be that type of good man. A man who would save everyone. But if my grandmother knew where I was driving from and why I had been there, my light would go out, too. From savior to drug dealer, just like my uncles. Just like their fathers. Just like my father. Having perfect grades, being an athlete, my position on student government, the long hours I worked at Red Lobster to make barely anything—none of it would matter. She hated drugs nearly as much as she was afraid of white people. She knew both had taken everything from her, our family, and almost every family in the neighborhood. She wouldn't even let me go outside to play with the other kids when I was growing up. Like they were going to taint me or something. Maybe that's what happened to my uncles. "You better keep your nose in them books, ain't nothing for you out there."

Grandmommy still had a lot of faith in my uncles, especially after my uncle Butch died of cancer when I was younger. "You know your uncles aren't bad, right? They were just like you. You'll see, they'll be home soon." She wasn't wrong, they would come around, and when they did it reminded me how much more work I needed to put in. They were selfish, drug-addicted, drunks. It made me disgusted that she would compare them to me. They weren't dutiful, they weren't around, they weren't good men. I might have been driving home from doing the wrong things, but at least I had the right reasons. They had even been with white women, I would be shunned for even knowing white women. I hated my uncles, they should be out here with me. It doesn't have to be instead of me, I just want some help buying this house with the garden. (Relax. Put on "Devotion," you love that song.)

"Through devotiooooon blessed are the childrennnn . . ." (See. You love Earth, Wind & Fire.) Why couldn't they be my uncles? I'm sure they were taking care of their responsibilities. I used to dream about the—

[Sirens. Lights. Here. Now.]

(What's that?) What's that?

"Please, pull over."

A CASE FOR DECRIMINALIZING SEX WORK

As he was placing her in the back of the car she said, "So y'all can build your empire with my mother's body and her mother's body, but I can't make money off my own? That ain't capitalism!"

"Ma'am, if you want to sleep with these men and then pay these other men, that's your problem. But not on my watch," the officer responded.

She stared at him for a moment and then laughed. "Why the hell not? Y'all all pimps anyway! Every one of you is trying to tax things that ain't yours to tax."

My lens and understanding of capitalism and patriarchy as they affect women's bodies was informed by gangs, white people, and sex work, as I had direct or indirect contact with all three in the culture surrounding my life in urban poverty. The first two were part of a money and power dynamic I had been able to easily wrap my mind around since I was a child. There were those who were born into power and money, such as the white people my entire camp had to write "thank-you" letters to at the end of the summer for sponsoring us with their excess wealth to have an experience "unique to children in our circumstances." Then there were those who were born without power and money but found various ways to seize it, such as the gang members left standing after blood was spilled over streets and buildings named after the white people who sponsored me to go to summer camp.

But I couldn't understand how various instances of sex work fit into all of this, especially as it related to prostitution. I knew what prostitution was, conceptually, and how one could make money from it, but what confused me was the power dynamics. In all the films, television shows, and music that represented prostitution in some way, there was always a man involved, often known as a pimp. There were also pimps in my neighborhood, most of whom belonged to the local gangs. I knew they were pimps because just like in the movies and shows I saw, the same rotation of women would stand outside with a man until someone would drive up and the woman would leave with him. It was the only time white men passed through my neighborhood unless they were the police. The woman would be dropped off a few hours later, at which point she would hand the pimp a wad of cash, and after counting the money, he would give her a smaller wad back. In instances when he was displeased for whatever the reason may have been, he either would decide not to pay her or would strike her, though I didn't understand why. I would watch this all unfold from my bedroom window. How she made the money and why she deserved it made sense to me; the men wanted to pay for what she had to offer. But I couldn't understand how and why "the pimp" had power over her and the money when he hadn't done anything to earn either.

I remember being about twelve years old and secretly watching an HBO show about sex work late one night when my mother had fallen asleep. You know, those shows you would put on that you knew you weren't supposed to be watching, so you had to arrange a channel that was playing cartoons for when you pressed the "last" button on the remote control. Just in case your parents woke up. As in my view of the world through my window, I didn't understand the things I had seen and heard during the show. So, the next day on the bus to school I asked a few of the older students questions about it. Two of the responses to my questions are seared into my brain to this day.

The first was a response from a boy whose name I can't recall, but I remember him being very nice and approachable. The boy had large eyes that made it feel as if he was telling the truth whenever he spoke. He had told me that he knew about prostitution, so I asked, "Why do women pay pimps, if they are the ones having sex?" The boy responded very quickly and firmly, in a tone that spoke to his surprise that I didn't know something so basic and fundamental. "Because they have to. It's always been that way."

For me, being the inquisitive child I was, that answer wasn't good enough. "Okay. But why has it always been that way?" Before the boy could respond, a girl named Allison chimed in. I don't remember much about her either, other than the fact that she always wore her hair in a ponytail and girls were now allowed to play basketball with the boys during gym period because her mother had come to school and filed a complaint.

Allison simply said, "Because the men protect them." So I asked, "Protect them from who?"

"From other men," Allison responded.

In my more evolved and astute understanding since my days of learning about patriarchal structures of power, privilege, and criminality on the school bus, I have developed two thoughts on sex work, especially relating to prostitution, that I believe in firmly. The first is that women should have full agency and autonomy to do whatever they so please with their bodies. The second is that if you are safely providing a wanted service that doesn't harm others, there should be nothing illegal about doing so. Anything else is utterly hypocritical in a capitalistic society where the "have-nots" are lauded for creating avenues of entrepreneurship, so long as they check the boxes of what we praise through the filters of white supremacy and patriarchy.

Though it comes as no surprise that my view on sex work is not shared by some, I find it interesting that "some" at times includes feminists. Some feminists believe that sex work itself is a patriarchal structure and to "protect" sex workers we must end the demand for sex work, meaning stricter laws to harshly criminalize clients, who are often men. This is the view of people who find sex work to be a physical embodiment of the patriarchy.

Those who view sex work as demeaning or degrading to women often view all women who do sex work as victims. I believe this lens upholds patriarchy in three key ways. First, it assumes that every woman who engages in sex work doesn't enjoy herself, which is an inherently patriarchal act of taking a woman's agency and autonomy. Second, the sex work industry includes a spectrum of people, many of whom have "clients" who are not or don't identify as men. Third, this lens ignores the reality that some people making a living through sex work are doing so because they lack employment opportunities, often as the result of other aspects of the patriarchy and white supremacy. Black trans women are a clear example of this situation. Simply wanting to end sex work doesn't resolve these issues for those who may be surviving thanks to it or find it liberating and enjoyable. It also erases the men who are engaged in sex work, who often don't face the same victimization and dangers as women.

The idea that sex work is a violation of women's rights speaks directly to issues of respectability politics and the policing of a woman's ability to make choices for herself, especially when those choices exist in opposition to narrow beliefs about morality and sexual freedom. For some, sex is a testament to how much they love someone, for others it's meant to be given to a person you intend to marry, and then there are people who simply believe sex is just sex, a physical act that makes a person feel good.

But treating sexuality as if it's some sacred thing to be reserved for love or marriage should not be imposed on others if that is not a person's preference. People should have complete freedom to do whatever they want sexually as long as they're not hurting others and have consent.

As authors, sex workers, and activists Juno Mac and Molly Smith have said,

> Anti-prostitution feminism is a place where men can participate in flinging slurs like "holes," "whores," "orifices," and "cum dumpsters" at sex workers—and call it feminist analysis. It's a place where men who consider themselves feminist-aligned can patronize and dismiss prostitute women, as men have done for centuries. It's a place where a police officer can rifle through the bathroom bin at a sex worker's flat, retrieve blood-soaked tampons, publish photographs of them in his memoir (with a touching dedication to sex workers he has met in his work: "this is my attempt to describe your reality"), and still be treated like a feminist activist.

There is only one absolute truth about sex work. As currently constructed in America, it can be extremely dangerous for everyone involved, especially women. Not because the act of pleasure in exchange for monetary gain is inherently dangerous, but rather because its criminality has created a culture in which it must exist in the shadows, which lends itself to danger. This leads me to the question I feel anyone who wants to tear down patriarchal structures should be asking rather than shaming the industry altogether: "How do we make sure that sex workers are safe and have equity within this industry?" It's the same question at the root of why many sex workers support complete decriminalization of their work as a means of protecting women, narrowing wealth gaps, and eradicating many of the work's dangerous pitfalls.

Forms of legal sex work already exist and are very lucrative for those engaged in them. Take OnlyFans, a content subscription service that gives creators the opportunity to monetize their engagement by charging "fans," who subscribe to their pages or pay to see specific content. Many people have used OnlyFans as a means of practicing sex work, and in some cases have earned millions of dollars doing so. During the Covid-19 pandemic, many women praised the service for giving them an opportunity to make extra money, and some have said it kept them from being homeless after losing their jobs.

If the true goal is to protect women and to dismantle parts of the patriarchy, then in the instance of sex work, we best do that by decriminalizing the sex work industry. By creating policies that protect and empower women and others engaging in sex work, we do far more good than the harm being done by shaming and endangering an entire industry of people.

VIEW (BY NOVELL JORDAN)

And then the author told his younger cousin, I see you.
I have seen you since you were born, and as you get to
know you, I will get to know you. For that opportunity,
I love you.

Do you see me?
I ask my parents. I was boy before anything else; before smart,
 before fast, before handsome, talented, educated.
Before Black.
Before bi.
I was boy. Your boy. Your small, wailing boy.
I know you say you love me,
"Forever and always," "unconditionally,"
But I fear one day that will cease.
That I will not be your boy anymore.
That you would not want me to be your boy
Anymore.
And I am afraid. Deeply afraid.
Do you see me?
I ask the first girl I've ever loved. We were the same, but I did not
 know. We were young.
You revered our people, brandished our flag, and spoke your truth.

I admired you.

Through you I learned that I am still man

even when I do not appear as those men around me.

I did not know myself

But found courage and truth from your words.

Thank you.

For cradling me when I couldn't find the thoughts to support myself.

When I couldn't bear the thoughts

Of knowing myself.

Do you see me?

I ask the first boy I've ever loved. I cannot say if you loved me back.

Do you remember the days we sat on your steps and talked for hours? You were out and I wasn't. I was frightened but you eased my fear. The bliss of novelty.

There was potential in us though I've grown, considerably, since then.

We lived everything but a fairy tale.

When I hungered for warmth, you force-fed me

ice-coated exclusion.

We were adolescents.

You taught me much about what is and what isn't love.

I'm happy we didn't last.

Do you see me?

I ask masculinity. You are not who they say you are. You are much more than

A template, a pre-cut frame, expectations.

You are unique.

My experiences and paradigms are your foundation.

You are no longer daunting. I pride myself on your creation.

You are what I, and only I, make of you.

Therefore you are

Man,

Me,

Despite my deviation from worldly boundaries.

Do you see me?

I ask my memory. When they ask "when did you know" you reply,

Always and Never.

There was no turning point,

no climax, no epiphany

no moment, no event

no trauma

no shame

It just has been.

It always has been.

Do you see me?

I ask humanity. Have I hidden well enough?

You've created a space in which the "wrong" label trumps

Human.

Am I not you?

Each person, a culmination of their limited

Encounters and exposures.

Immerse yourself in fallibility.

I have ceased attempting to convince you

that my existence is

Legitimate.

It is.

Do you see me?

I ask my creator. You planted me in tainted soil and yet I've
bloomed.

I wonder

Do you chuckle as you watch me play with the burning cards
you've placed in my

Cherubic palms?

I, still, thank you.

Because with gloved fingers my

Existential dexterity could not have

Danced with the very flames that

tried to burn me.

Do you see me?

I ask love. My version of you is not celebrated. You are reduced to
mere sex and heresy.

But that is not you.

I've learned that you can look different,

Sound different,

Feel different, and be real.

I've learned that though you may appear different

You are always the same;

A fundamental emotion. Unavoidable.

I've crafted my own meaning

my own Understanding

Of you.

Do you see me?

I ask myself. Do you see now?

Who you are.

You are vinyls and rose petals, funk and jazz, hoodies and button-
downs, Frank Ocean and the internet, choreography and high
notes, fast cars and loud music, parties and vogue, politics and
current events, cuffed pants and tucked shirts, comic books and
house music.

Mosaic child

You are

A life span, living only the way you believe to be correct.

Like everyone else.

You are a person. Nothing more, nothing less.

You are duality, complexity, simplicity,

An identity only you need to validate.

You are not concerned with labels because

he/him means nothing when we are ash and our planet is no more.

Your identity is not to be tested.

It does not need to be proven, verified, or justified to any like mortal
beings. You are comfortable.

With the knowledge that the only trial you must pass

Is your own.

Be yourself.

Do you remember how the masses thanked you for being yourself?

In the short time that I am allowed to walk on Her beautiful Earth,

I chose an aerial view atop cumulus clouds of Acceptance.

I place my seat under solar rays of Peace,

relax my shoulders on tender waves of Tranquillity, and allow
Love-Filled currents to carry my

Soul.
I want to live happy.
I want to live human.
I want to live free.
Like you.

WHO CARRIES THE HATRED?

There was something inside of him. Something ugly and corrosive, which he caught from his brother, who caught it from their mother, who caught it from her father. A germ. One that made no sense, with origins that couldn't be traced. The infection started in the brain by telling them lies, then it spread to the heart by making it black, and finally it spread to the hands, feet, and mouth, making them do things without reason. The virus was unnatural, unlike what it aimed to destroy.

I was watching *Wedding Crashers* and a few other early 2000s comedies and I noticed an extremely problematic trend. Each of the movies had numerous moments of overt homophobia for the sake of trying to make audiences laugh. It's not that I hadn't seen these movies before, but I suppose homophobia was so normalized to me in the past that I didn't even recognize it when it was happening right in front of me. Not to say I'm perfect at recognizing it now, but I do have a much more watchful eye. For example, many of my friends grew up with homophobic tendencies, especially in the language they use, though I'm sure none of them would consider themselves homophobes. Now I often find myself having to call them out and explain how and why things they are saying that have been a part of their everyday vocabulary since they were children are actually reinforcing homophobic ideologies and rhetoric. It isn't always easy, and has put me in a position where I have fewer friends today than I did before. But if it means that others feel safer around me and the people I vouch for, then it's worth it.

For the next few days I was thinking about what other instances of homophobia I had missed when I was younger, and I remembered just how pervasive it was not only in movies, but in music and language. I won't repeat some of the things that were said, but homophobia was so ingrained that I recall it being a part of everyday vernacular in my middle and high schools. I could make a case that every few minutes in a conversation there was something said by both men and women, heterosexual and not, that was homophobic. That same normalization of homophobia is still rampant, and so nuanced that many can't see it. The other night I was watching a Lakers game and one of their players, Kyle Kuzma, was wearing a necklace made of pearls. I didn't think anything of it, not until heading to social media to read the reactions to the team's surprising win over the Brooklyn Nets. When I went on Twitter, I was disgusted by what I saw (usually the case with Twitter).

Fox Sports host and former NFL player Shannon Sharpe had commented on Kuzma's pearls: "Did I just see Kuzma on the sideline wearing pearls? LAWD have mercy" (the comment also had emojis showing a man slapping his own forehead in frustration). His tweet received nearly seven hundred responses, most of which were disgustingly homophobic. But one person responded, "Shannon, why are you being homophobic?" to which over forty people responded in return with variations of "He isn't being homophobic." And "How is this homophobia?" I believe Kuzma identifies as heterosexual, but this is just a further reflection of how deep homophobia runs. A man who isn't gay can't even wear certain clothing or accessories because he will be perceived as "gay."

We have all been conditioned in heteronormativity, and that conditioning often manifests itself in deeply homophobic rhetoric and actions. It's unacceptable, and consciously or not, I've been a culprit myself. That's not to say I was ever a homophobe, but I was unknowingly perpetuating homophobia in my actions and inactions. The fact that you don't have to commit the seemingly overt acts of bigotry to uphold bigotry is an important concept. Much of society operates under the assumption that if people haven't said the word "nigger" or physically harmed a Black person, they aren't racist. But racism, like homophobia, and any other form of actionable ignorance, exists on a spectrum. Using a slur to refer to a gay man is not the same as assuming a gay man has an interest in fashion, but both are rooted in homophobia.

A lack of understanding or alignment regarding these spectrums is how many people absolve themselves of accountability for bigoted behaviors. Additionally, many bigoted behaviors and attitudes relating to the LGBTQ+ community are often believed to be held only by people who

- Never engaged in any non-heterosexual behaviors
- Believe those around them have negative views about the LGBTQ+ community
- Haven't had personal contact with the LGBTQ+ community
- Identify as heterosexual men
- Live in areas where negative sentiments about the LGBTQ+ community are often normalized, especially rural areas
- Are past the age of fifty
- Have not attended or graduated from college
- Hold conservative religious views

While studies have shown that many of these assumed demographics for homophobic behaviors and attitudes may be true, they are not exhaustive. Meaning that you can exist as the complete opposite of every one of the instances listed and still perpetuate homophobia.

If you've met one person from any community, they are in fact one person. A piece or part of anything fundamentally cannot truly be representative of the whole. The Black community, the disabled community, and the LGBTQ+ community are not monolithic. People within these groups may have some similar views or experiences, but they are also dynamic individuals who exist as themselves and should speak for no one but themselves. Our views are based on only three things: what we have learned, what we have been told, and what we have experienced. Views about the LGBTQ+ community are no different, and unfortunately, many people act solely on the basis of what they have been told rather than what they have learned or experienced. All three categories should be part of the process for us to develop any true assessment of, well, anything.

I recently learned that one of my uncles, who died when I was about ten years old, actually died of AIDS from sharing heroin needles. This surprised me because my grandmother had always told me he died of cancer. My other uncle told me she withheld the true information because she felt if people knew he died of AIDS, they would have thought he had been having sex with men. There was a very prevalent false narrative at the time that HIV/AIDS had been identified among and was spread solely by gay Black men. This is a complete and utter lie that propelled generations of homophobia. I had never considered my grandmother a bigoted person, she would have told you herself that she loved everyone, including the LGBTQ+ community. She wasn't a hateful person and was open and sympathetic to the plights and lives of others. But the reality was that as much as she believed she had love in her heart for those unlike herself, much of that love only pertained as long as they didn't extend into her own life. It's easy to not be bigoted when you aren't close to those you claim not to be bigoted toward.

Only 3.5 percent of Americans openly identify as belonging to the LGBTQ+ community, which means that most opinions on the group, good or bad, are not based on proximity. Growing up I remember men in the barbershop and in the neighborhood saying gay men were child molesters, mentally ill, and dangerous. These were such prevailing narratives that I recall when

I was a child my older cousin talking to her friend about my love for musical theater, to which her friend laughed and said, "He might be gay. But at least you'll have someone to go shopping with." At that moment I decided to stop enjoying musical theater, as I didn't want to be labeled "gay." Every fiber of my being wanted to experience what it was like to be treated as if I belonged, which was something that didn't come with being Black, poor, and fatherless. I couldn't let anyone add something else to the list. I might not have survived if they had. Which says a great deal about the people who did exist at similar intersections, and were also actually gay or bi.

This is why it's so important to address how we are all conditioned in the normalization of homophobia. By aligning specific behaviors, emotions, interests, and actions solely with this group we inherently do a disservice to ourselves as non-monolithic people. These false beliefs often create unneeded conscious or unconscious conflicts within ourselves if we deviate from the boxes in which we've placed ourselves and the LGBTQ+ community. If only gay men enjoy fashion, how many heterosexual men are ignoring their interest in fashion because of that false narrative? If only lesbians enjoy playing sports, how many heterosexual women have opted out of doing so, though they would like to play? If we allow a range of emotions to convey joy and sadness for only gay men and women, where does that leave a heterosexual man? Simply with their anger? We are repressing our full selves in service of hatred against others.

AS THEY RAMPAGE

*He never learned to cry, never learned to heal, never
learned to be happy, and never learned what is real.
Instead he learned to hunt, instead he learned to fight,
instead he learned to lie, instead he learned to cheat,
instead he learned to steal.*

    But above all he learned to shoot. So shoot he did.

Oh, how those beasts feed in the wild.
The hunt may make your stomach turn.
The slaughter may make your stomach turn . . .
THE CARNAGE SHOULD MAKE YOUR FUCKING
    STOMACH TURN.
The Massas say,
Ahem.
The Masters say,
there is more where that came from.
And on the eighth day,
the Masters spared no one.
No one said,
"Good morning, teacher!"
No one's someone marched,
until their feet bled.

But the beasts must feed.
And on the eighth day,
the Masters spared no one.
No one said,
"I'll be in aisle five."
No one's someone wept,
until their tears washed them into the river.
But the beasts must feed.
And on the eighth day,
the Masters spared no one.
No one said,
"I'm going to see if they want to dance."
No one's someone slept,
until they saw no one again.
But the beasts must feed.
And on the eighth day,
the Masters spared no one.
No one said,
"I'm reading a poem."

THE EPIDEMIC OF RAPE CULTURE

"Ayy, what's your name?"

She can't go to the dog park.

"Maybe we should hang out outside of work sometime."

She can't go to the office.

"You're wearing those jeans! Looking good!"

She can't ride this train home anymore.

"Where are you going this late, sweetheart?"

She can't jog here after the streetlights come on.

"Come on, it's just a kiss."

She can't go to dinner with him again.

"Well, you wanted it before. So I figured you wanted it again."

She can't stay married to him anymore.

I was at the dog park recently and there just happened to be only men in the park. Eventually, a woman came jogging up to the entrance with her dog. As she began to open the gate, she looked around to see who was in the park, then decided not to come in and walked away. As she walked away, one of the men said loudly, "There's room in here for an ass that nice!" She ignored him and kept walking. He then said, "I'm joking!

Come on in!" Then she started jogging away with her dog, running much faster than she had been when jogging toward the park.

Immediately as she started running, the man turned to the man sitting next to him and said, "What's she acting like that for? My snake won't bite unless—unless she wants it to." The man sitting next to him began to laugh. I walked over to the men and said, "Are you fucking serious? What the fuck is your problem?" The man was utterly taken aback; he couldn't understand what I was referring to. "What? My dog do some dumb shit to your dog?"

"No. Why were you harassing her like that? What's your fucking problem?" I responded.

"Oh! That? I was just having a little fun. I'm from a time where we could have fun. Stop acting like a [gay slur]," the man responded. To which I ended up telling him we could step outside the dog park or take our dogs home and meet afterward. He didn't oblige, and the reality was that even if I beat him to a bloody pulp and dragged him to her doorstep as a tribute, it wouldn't fix anything. She would still have experienced the trauma, would likely be afraid to come back to the only dog park in our neighborhood, and the other men who didn't take issue with his harassment would still find him relatable enough to laugh with. He was right, he was from a time where they could have that type of misogynistic "fun." A time where I learned much of the same, and had it not been for being raised solely by women who I had watched live through similar instances, I might have done the same thing. The problem is that not much has really changed since that time, as much as some might like to think so.

Rape culture is everywhere. It exists at work, on television, on the way to the store, in our homes, in music, online, and in our romantic relationships. Paternalistic beliefs that women are inferior to men have become so ingrained in our society that objectifying women through sexual harassment and abuse are often more normalized than combating these issues.

There are many reasons why rape culture persists, and the media is a large one. It has not only normalized sexual harassment and abuse, but also desensitized our culture to the impact and implications of rape culture, thus creating an obstacle in preventing it. I can recall many films in which a young woman is reprimanded by her parents or some other adult figure for being what was thought of as scantily clad. In almost every instance, the young woman is told that her clothing will invite wrong assumptions about her and could ultimately lead to her inviting unwanted, and potentially deadly, behavior. Rather than the writers of those moments opting to create scenes that demonstrate the importance of talking to young men about how not to engage with a young woman in an abusive way, they place the blame, guilt, and responsibility at the feet of the would-be victims. This is also known as victim blaming.

The very nature of a woman's rights has been distorted and bastardized by patriarchal thinking that aims to erase any existence of women outside of that which benefits and/or is controlled by a man. This control has been actualized within the media and law as the core respect for a woman's personhood has been denied. If a woman wasn't even a full legal human being in the eyes of US law until a few decades ago, why wouldn't a young woman be raped for wearing a short dress?

In the imaginations of many men, women are property. These same men are often the ones who make and uphold the laws, write the television shows, shoot the films, pen the books, and manage the companies that treat women as such. You can't hurt property, property doesn't deserve respect, you can't rape property. Property has no control over its own body. The greatest and most pervasive tool of oppressors has always been to erase the humanity of the oppressed.

There are many ways in which this phenomenon exists, but what often comes to mind is how men catcall women. I've always found catcalling disgusting, largely because I had to watch my mother deal with it so much when I was a child. But even though I've never been a proponent of catcalling, I can't deny how common it was around me most of my life and how complicit I was as other men and boys were doing it.

I still recall how normalized it was for us as young men to stand outside and whistle, yell, and even grab women passing by who were found attractive. I knew I wasn't interested in doing those things, but I think that was primarily because I was embarrassed when my mother was subjected to the same treatment. Not because I felt bad for my mother or the other women who were dealing with catcalling. Which is likely why I was always so complicit, because I wasn't being an ally, I was just self-centered. I'm not even sure who taught me or any of the people I was around that catcalling was okay; it was simply something that happened, and doing it was such a common occurrence that I was looked at as if I was odd for not engaging in it.

Access to women's bodies and time has always been considered rights that men have and deserve. I remember many instances in which men would catcall a woman and only stop if the woman told them that she was taken or related to some specific man the group knew. As if a woman is only entitled to respect when qualified by her proximity to a man.

The way the media depicts sexual harassment only exacerbates rape culture. In *The Wood*, one of my favorite films growing up, three teenage boys make a bet on which of them will lose their virginity first. This wager culminates in the friends pressuring their girlfriends and young women they barely know about having sex with them. I distinctly remember a scene in which one of the boys says to his girlfriend, "Why you frontin'? You let Terry bone. I know I look better . . ." thinking that her having had sex with someone else meant he was entitled to have sex with her. There's another scene in which the group places a different wager, on who can first touch the butt of a girl in school. One of the boys gladly does so a few days later on the playground. While the young woman does become angry at her butt being touched, and her older brother does end up punching the boy in the face, years later the boy and the young woman end up becoming best friends and losing their virginity to one another. They even end up together as adults. Happy ending for everyone, rape culture and all.

I was ten years old when *The Wood* was released and about eleven years old the first time I saw it. For a young man with no other men around as positive figures, a coming-of-age story about young men slightly older than myself was very impactful. So impactful in fact that some months later I found myself agreeing to a bet with one of the popular boys in school on whether I would touch a young woman's butt in my class. As in the movie, I happily obliged, and was ultimately sent to the principal's office for doing so. The principal, a woman, let me off without so much as a suspension or an explanation of why what I did was wrong because I was a good student and because "boys will be boys," as she told me in her office.

I was even younger when I watched *The Sandlot* for the first time. It's a film that for many is an American pop culture staple, but until recently I didn't realize how deeply it normalizes rape culture.

On a turbulent early morning flight, I decided to rewatch the film to calm my nerves, and the first half hour or so was just as I remembered from my childhood. A classic tale of boyhood friendship and trying to fit in. But then something happened that I hadn't recalled.

The group of boys decide to visit a local pool where a young white woman named Wendy, who seems to be a few years older than the boys, is the lifeguard on duty. The boys are immediately mesmerized by her, but none more than Michael, also known as "Squints." He is so mesmerized in fact that he devises a plan to kiss Wendy.

Though he can't swim, Squints decides to jump in the deep end of the pool, which causes a frenzy amongst his friends and everyone else at the pool, including Wendy, who must now attempt to save Squints's life. Wendy dives in the pool and drags the unconscious Squints out, then proceeds to give mouth-to-mouth resuscitation. Eventually Squints regains consciousness, unbeknownst to Wendy, but his friends realize he's awake once Squints opens his eyes to wink at them before grabbing Wendy's head and forcing her lips to stay pressed against his. She eventually pulls her head away (no one helps her) and kicks the boys out.

As the boys exit the pool, Wendy heads back to her lifeguard station and watches the boys walk outside the pool gate. Squints stares at her through a gate with a look like a puppy that found its way into a bag of groceries and made a mess. Of course, you're mad about the groceries, but how mad can you be at such a cute dog with yogurt all over its face? Wendy responds to Squints's look in the same way, breaking the stern stare she was giving him and eventually smiling as if he's a puppy who just doesn't know any better because boys will be boys.

I wonder what that scene taught a generation of children such as myself who watched the film in our most formative years. When I googled "issues with *The Sandlot*" to see whether anyone had noticed this scene or others, all I found were articles about illogical details such as fireworks providing enough light to play baseball at night. Either this moment of sexual assault was so normalized that people didn't realize it took place or it was so normalized that it was deemed not worth discussing.

These are the types of moments that make lyrics such as "I know you want it, /But you're a good girl, /The way you grab me, /Must wanna get nasty, /Go ahead, get at me" and "What do they make dreams for, /When you got them jeans on?" from Robin Thicke's 2013 hit song "Blurred Lines" seem acceptable.

In other words, when a woman says no, she actually means yes, according to these lyrics. They also mean that a flirtatious woman wishes to engage in sexual intercourse, and there are limits to a woman's right to change her mind. Ultimately, it is a man that decides whether a woman wants to or will have sex. "Blurred Lines" is an apt title for a song epitomizing rape culture, a song which has over 500 million listens on Spotify.

Rape culture is ingrained in every aspect of our society, and it starts young. Children are being indoctrinated into it and thus perpetuating it as they grow older. It's at the center of why Tarana Burke's #MeToo movement is so important and why influential people such as Harvey Weinstein, R. Kelly, Bill Cosby, and Jeffrey Epstein were able to abuse countless women and girls without fear of condemnation. Not only did they use their own individual power to protect themselves, but they used the patriarchal systems surrounding them, all of which were designed to protect them.

Gwyneth Paltrow first worked with Harvey Weinstein when she starred in the film *Emma*, in 1996. Before she began filming, she met with Weinstein at the Peninsula Beverly Hills hotel. Paltrow said he placed hands on her, then suggested they go upstairs to a bedroom to give each other "massages." "I was a kid, I was signed up, I was petrified," she said. "I thought he was going to fire me."

Unfortunately, these same influences and systems condition us all to uphold rape culture, even those from groups most victimized by it. This is seen in the thoughts of other women, which Weinstein's attorneys used to contradict his victims and exonerate him. Fashion designer Donna Karan had defended Weinstein, saying he had done wonderful things, and considered whether the women had "asked for it." She eventually apologized for the comments. Similarly, actress Lindsay Lohan said in a quickly deleted Instagram video: "I feel very bad for Harvey Weinstein right now . . . I don't think it's right what's going on. I think Georgina needs to take a stand and be there for her husband. He's never harmed me or did anything to me. We've done several movies together. I think everyone needs to stop. I think it's wrong. So, stand up."

This is not to say the two women are at fault for Weinstein's actions, but it is an example of how even those oppressed by patriarchy may also be conditioned to uphold it.

Ending all manifestations of rape culture should be at the forefront of the minds of people who want to protect women, but it will take both men and women to do so. We must unpack and unlearn the ways in which we've been conditioned and hold accountable the systems that are perpetuating these beliefs.

WOMANIZER

Trying to steal parts of women won't make you whole,
and it certainly won't make you a man.

　　Burn me down with my lies of milk and honey,
ashes to ashes and dust to dust in the wind
carried to peaks of monuments built to myself.
Ships meant to sail into never,
the wind of unfamiliar respect at the back
of supposed notches tying me to the mast.
Don't fight back. Nor run from this,
as we ran from me to the men we pretended to be.
Just tell my mother I love her.
　　"Just her, is why you are here."
　　It's true.
Boys on strings telling tall tales
of not being her past and better than her future.
Barbershop folklore. Locker room fables.
Echoes of offered nothingness in hollow halls,
filled with rooms of shortcomings,
disguised as remnants of trust and bodies.
Surrounded by women, alone is the boy
pretending to be a man.

I COME APART

The wind howled and thunder boomed in the distance. Everyone ran inside to escape the oncoming storm. As they did, he took off his sandals and walked down to the water. He wanted to feel the sand between his toes one last time. Then he was alone.

As he stood there, lightning cracked on the horizon and the ocean washed the sand off his feet. Then came the rain.

He stepped into the water, and you couldn't tell, but he began to cry.

You:

I don't know of a way to refer to you other than as a weight I no longer want to carry. You are less a name to me than a feeling—or a hardship. There was a time when I called you "I don't like it" and "please stop" so much that I now struggle to remember your actual name. Nonetheless, I'm writing to you now in order to reclaim the pieces of me you stole long ago, so that I may eventually call you nothing.

For nearly three decades, instead of dreaming, I spent my time lost in nightmares about whether you had more pieces of me than

I had of myself. About whether this body and the life it occupied was just a shell, and the bones that made up my best parts were somewhere in the closet with the rest of your skeletons. On many nights when I couldn't cry myself to sleep, I would stare at the ceiling wondering whether I'd rather see you the next day or die. There's no appropriate age for someone to forget how to smile and laugh, but I was so young. I had barely been here long enough to truly learn to do either.

Time washes away so much, but never the things you want it to. I still remember your red lipstick. So much so that my fiancée, who loves red lipstick, doesn't wear it anymore. She understands some of the hurt. But she doesn't know it hurt me so much that I mastered being outside of my body when I saw you put it on. That it hurt so much that I just recently began to stop equating a kiss with a violation. I refused to cry. You could take everything else, but the tears were mine. I think I was saving those tears, waiting for my chance to float away.

Sometimes I think back to how fascinated I was by the children at school who were different than I was. They always seemed so happy and careless. I'd sit by myself at recess and watch them, much like a farmer watching a herd peacefully graze, knowing they would eventually be devoured by someone. But I didn't know what their future held. Maybe I just hoped someone would face something similar to what happened to me. Not because I wanted anyone to have to feel the pain I was feeling, but because I felt so alone, and wanted someone to understand.

I know it hurts, but keep going.

Someone else who was being told lies that they were "lucky" or that they should be "thankful" to have those experiences so early. You gaslighted me to the pits of hell.

Those moments in which my ears, my eyes, my tongue, and my hands lost all sense, I lost the ability to distinguish angels from demons. So much so that I began to fear nearly all women. I was terrified of what a woman could do in the shadows that no one seemed to realize. Terrified for the young boys in class with childhood crushes on young girls, having no idea of the darkness they might sow. The same young girls my classmates called me "weird" for not being interested in. I didn't act like the other boys in school or in my neighborhood, so I didn't have many friends. I was more concerned with surviving than being someone's sweetheart. Although it didn't matter much, when you're suffering through secrets such as I was, you learn to be close friends with yourself.

During an interview recently, I was asked what the best moment of my life was—I lied. What I said was that it was the moment I proposed to my fiancée. But that's what I wish it was. In reality, the best moment of my life, the one in which I've felt the most utter and complete joy, was a Sunday afternoon shortly after my tenth birthday. My mother was sorting through her bills that morning and trying to figure out where she was going to find extra money since our rent had increased. She sat me down and said, "You're mature for your age. I think I can trust you to stay home by yourself after school from now on. It would really help me if I didn't have to pay someone to watch you." I immediately told her that I understood and she could trust me. I proceeded to calmly walk to my room and slowly close the door, then I lay on my bed and smiled as I hadn't smiled in years.

That may have been the first time in history living in poverty saved someone's life.

Most of the end was unceremonious. You left me alone for a few weeks after my mother told you she would no longer need the services she thought you were providing. After she told you I would soon be free. But the last day, the day I had looked forward to for years— that day was the worst of them. That was the day when you took my future, even if you wouldn't be there to see it.

"Something to remember me by when you're doing the things I taught you with the rest of them."

I do remember—every single moment. There was no escaping my body that day. By the time you were done, I felt as if I would never truly escape you. As I stepped out of your home for the last time, I considered walking straight to the medicine cabinet. I didn't want this body anymore; it was broken by a life that was rotten. I understand the plague of society's dark secrets and despicable nature that would make a child with so little life lived wish they could be rid of it all so soon. "But what about your mother?" "What about your grandmother?"

I wouldn't let you destroy them, too. Which is the only reason I'm still here.

The next few years are somewhat of a blur. I suppose for a long time I viewed most things and people in my life through the lens of my trauma, which made it nearly impossible to experience anything or anyone in a healthy or productive way. I do know there were moments I found some semblance of happiness, but never wholeness. The older I became, the more my lack of interest in women became a point of concern for those around me. "He hasn't even had a little girl-

friend yet. You think he's gay? He's probably gay. He's into a bunch of things gay kids are into," I recall overhearing my older cousin say as I secretly listened. To which my other cousin jokingly replied, *"I know. He does walk funny, doesn't he?"* Then they shared a laugh together, at the expense of their cousin and all the boys who might actually have been gay.

Had I not still been saving my tears, I probably would have cried for the first time in years that day. Instead, I decided to prove them wrong. But doing so nearly swallowed whatever light I may have had left.

Though I learned to enjoy being alone, and many people didn't have an interest in knowing me anyway, there were two boys who had become almost like brothers to me. So much so that before we got to high school, I shared with them some of the secrets I had been keeping. I was finally ready to find some light in all of the darkness I had been holding in. To my surprise, they couldn't wrap their minds around the idea that what you did, what you had stolen, was a curse. All they saw in their hormone-and-media-driven lust was a gift. One whose occurrence they decided to share with everyone they knew after I told them. It was this supposed gift that made me popular with many young women. To them I wasn't broken or hurt—I was "advanced." Even when I would have preferred to be seen as something needing to be fixed.

Some days, I don't know what's more of a curse. What you did to me, or that society both fetishizes and sexualizes Black bodies so much that most Black children aren't given the space to be victims. I was one of those children, a Black boy treated as if I had received a gift by being "advanced," by being adultified. So rarely do we have *conversations about how many Black men say they have been sexually active since they were children. Conversations about the fact that they were just boys and these Black men were actually raped. I was raped.*

For all of the Black girls and boys inside us who will never get to confront their abusers, I am here to hold you accountable. You raped me.

What you took from me left a void, and like far too many others, instead of filling it with healing I tried to fill it with pieces of other people. The older I became, the more I tried to run away from my trauma and fear of women. I developed a hatred for women, which I confused with healing. My truth is that I'm still unpacking years of misogyny, sexism, and toxic masculinity. Living through trauma became my excuse for forcing trauma on others. But the truth is that the only person I feared was a vulnerable and hurt version of myself, who also happened to be the only person I hated as well. I refused to accept that you molesting me had damaged me, because that would also mean accepting that I needed to be healed. It would confirm that I needed to be fixed. The great triumph of most people who sexually abuse others is that they circumvent accountability by making the victim believe they were at fault. You created a world where "I shouldn't have" was always louder than "she shouldn't have."

It wasn't my fault. It wasn't my fault. It wasn't my fault. It wasn't my fault.

I stopped hating myself a very short while ago, just long enough to begin building myself a boat. Not to sail away from my pain, but rather to sail toward it. If I don't confront my hurt, I'll never have the pleasure of finding out that I'm not actually broken. I'm just waiting to fill the voids left by pain with the joy that only more life can bring. To do that, I have to let go.

Holding on to what a woman in her fifties started doing to me when I was eight years old has conceived nothing but agony. Agony for myself, and agony for those whom I used as ports in a storm of sorrow that evolved into selfishness. Destruction begets nothing but more destruction, which is what I'm sure led us here—and why I forgive you.

I forgive you for how you might have suffered and wished you were dead, which ultimately made you hurt me so. I forgive you for the pieces of me you stole in order to fill the voids I'm sure your pain left. Because in forgiving you I reclaim those pieces, not for me, but for my fiancée and our future children.

In these very words, in this very sentence, I feel whole. I feel light. I'm crying. These tears that I refused to let you take. These tears I've been holding on to for all these years.

They were all to help me float away from there to now. To this very moment, this place where I am ready to move on.

Goodbye, nothing.

Sincerely,
Someone who will soon be whole

PURITY AND GRACE

"The boy loves to dance, Joe!"

"I don't care, ain't no son of mine dancing. He needs to be playing football or basketball, just like I did. Like the other boys!"

"Why? So he can hate it and resent us? He should play football like you did? You became a dentist! What's the problem with dancing?"

"It's not what young boys do! Not unless—"

"Unless what, Joe? Say it. You're a bigot, just like your father."

"I'm nothing like that man! I'm just saying that—"

"You're just saying that your daddy beat you senseless because he caught you playing in your mother's jewelry box. You and him aren't much different."

Mr. Zawel,

If someone is lucky they'll meet a few people in their life who seismically shift their entire world. Sometimes we don't even realize it's happening because even the most important people are often merely seasons of our lives. Colorful fall leaves gone with the winds that brought them in.

The same wind that has taken you home now.

Regardless how long or short the person's time is with us, at some point we come to the realization that they are a part of our DNA. Woven into the very fabric of who we are. Part of the code that makes you—you.

In that way, I am somewhat of a living testament to the seasons of your life.

Although we were not blood, you are as much a part of me as if we were pulled right off the same tree. I find it difficult to admit both to myself and publicly that at the very core of many of my talents and interests lives a white, middle-aged, Jewish drama teacher. This is not meant as a personal affront to you, but rather a projection of my trauma, and an indictment of the society that caused it. A reflection of how I constantly aim to step as far away from whiteness as possible, for my own emotional and physical safety. The same whiteness that has attempted to step on, over, and through me my entire life.

In the many decades since, you introduced me to musical theater, gave me the opportunity to pen scripts, and taught me to speak from my diaphragm. Taught me to speak from my diaphragm. TAUGHT ME TO SPEAK FROM MY DIAPHRAGM.

But—I have changed.

I'm fully aware that is to be expected of anyone growing older, but I am talking about something deeper. I have seen far more winters than summers, far more cold deaths than new lives of spring. My soul has changed—my spirit has changed.

But before I was this man writing to you now with an exhausted pen, I was a wide-eyed hopeful boy. The boy you knew, the boy you taught, the boy you made believe he could do anything. But anything *is often a privilege and luxury not afforded to many of us.*

Not to the Black boy from low-income housing who wants to be a Broadway star, not to the disabled teenager who wants to be a model, not to the trans woman who wants to safely go to a bar with her friends. Our society doesn't afford most these luxuries—it barely affords survival.

The question I asked myself when deciding to begin this project was "how did I get here?" It's the question I keep coming back to, and the question that I'm hoping readers ask themselves. Like white supremacy, the patriarchy and all of its manifestations are learned and developed. Therefore, they can be unlearned and undeveloped. But to do that, we must understand where, why, and how.

Which leads me back to Stephen Zawel and Frederick Joseph.

You may be the singular white person I have ever met who truly saw my possibility. Not my potential, as that word represents an extension of some prior demonstrated talent or ability. But my possibility, a simple extension of the imagination. Seeing raw material and giving it the space and opportunity to become whatever it may.

Not my possibility solely as a Black person, but my possibility as a whole being.

It's sad to consider, really. A man more than thirty years old living in a white country, having been taught by countless white educators, hired by countless white managers, and yet only one person knew (or admitted) how deep my well actually is.

Who might I have been had I but a few more people in a position to give me the space to become? What other mountains might I have climbed, if not for the avalanches of educators so hell-bent on up-holding white supremacy?

There are far too many others suffering from oppression asking similar questions. All of us, children raised in the same house. Yet being taught to forget that many of us share a room.

We are led to believe ourselves strangers, but this has never been true. How might we share an abusive landlord, drink the same poison, be beat with the same switch and still be strangers? Because when the landlord's arm is tired, he wants me to use the same switch he beat me with to batter my brother, to weld my sister. When we do that enough, we confuse each other for the landlord as opposed to kin with the common goals of freedom and possibility.

The common goal of escaping this house.

Over the years, I've wondered whether you had similar conversations with yourself about your people. White people. About the way they demand, destroy, and sin.

I like to think you must have, because the only way that people with privilege can avoid further damaging those without the same privileges is by being intentional about their actions. But I suppose I'll never know. As I was too afraid and embarrassed to reach out to you during those many passing seasons.

I was afraid that maybe the reality of a white Jewish man didn't live up to the mythology of a young Black boy who stopped dabbling in white false hopes and saviorism as he became a man. I was embarrassed because you would ask me why I didn't pursue a career in the musicals, which I loved so much. The answer, while very much rooted in my circumstances as a poor Black person, would also force me to be honest with myself about how much of it was also rooted in homophobia.

The boy who went with his grandmother on a school trip to see his first Broadway musical, Phantom of the Opera, and swore he would be "the first Black phantom," gave up on that dream. Instead he sat in an audience fifteen years later and watched Norm Lewis, another Black man, accomplish his dream. Because musical theater was "gay."

As a young man, I wanted to pass the eye test for people's heteronormative gaze. Which meant catching footballs and hitting people as opposed to memorizing the lines to one of Sondheim's works. I barely had the strength to fight white supremacy, let alone heteronormativity and toxic masculinity.

There was one night, however, that I nearly decided to reach out. Until what I felt was an insightful fear stopped me.

"He has a thousand dreams that won't come true, /you know that he believes in them /and that's enough for you."

A few years ago, I found myself in my living room listening to The King and I soundtrack thinking back on being in fifth grade, when you asked our drama class what that line meant.

I don't believe I had an answer then, but I do now. My answer is: a good life.

The lines represent a good life, one filled with so many dreams they aren't all attainable, but the beauty is that we endeavor to make it so. The magic of life is in the attempt.

I thought about finding you online that night and emailing you my answer, some twenty years later. But as I continued listening to the soundtrack, I began to reconsider the story line and characters you introduced me to so long ago. Suddenly, what was once simply a feel-good musical was now the consummate tale of colonialism.

A British widow travels to a foreign land to instill Western education, culture, and values in people of color who are portrayed as barbarians. Let's not even start on Yul Brynner, a white Russian-born man who won multiple awards for donning body tanner to play a person of color in the show and the film.

Ultimately, I decided not to contact you. For my own sake, I would let you remain a myth.

I remember being frustrated that night after thinking more about the problematic musical. How could he? Wondering how someone so seemingly thoughtful about my humanity and possibility couldn't see how wrong this was.

Maybe because too often we don't account for human error in those trying to do the right thing.

A few years after that night, I was thinking about Lorraine Hansberry's A Raisin in the Sun, and about who first introduced me to the play. I realized—you did. You also introduced our class to August Wilson, Langston Hughes, and countless other Black playwrights and writers who I draw upon even now to speak to you.

I took some time and considered my disappointment over The King and I. While judgment against a white Jewish man who consistently demonstrated ill will would be understandable, the same could be said of further investigation of a Jewish white man who had done the opposite.

So often we forget how to give grace, even when we've received it ourselves.

Ultimately, you may have not lived up to the myth, but I wouldn't know unless I faced you. Sadly, I never had the chance. I learned on a cold rainy April day as I searched for you online that you had passed just a few months before.

Everything around us is a show. Every last part of it. Filled with lights, stage managers, actors, and directors. The house we were all born in is one of its greatest props.

We all play a role in it. I believe you knew this. I believe you saw that a problematic role had been written for me: "the Black boy." A simple role that didn't have many lines and focused more on physicality.

Run. Jump. Shoot. Dance. Fight. Die.

A step up from the role of "the Black boy" a few generations earlier. Which wasn't much different from the role of "the Black man" during that time.

Plow. Lift. Pick. Run. Die.

But those roles pale in comparison to the expectations of people playing "the Black girl" and "the Black woman."

Run. Jump. Shoot. Dance. Fight. Cook. Clean. Give birth. Give support. Be quiet. Speak up. Be perfect. Be imperfect. Die.

I believe you knew it's a terrible show. In your own ways, you did what you could to help me and others outgrow it. Gave the space to imagine and improvise onstage, which could lead to new roles.

You were a great storyteller. You let yourself be lost in the lives of others. Watched, listened, learned—got out of the way. Allowing for growth, change, and evolution to inspire their own work and worldview.

You were a master storyteller, whether you realized it or not. I am learning to be one in my own right, doing what I can to effect change so that those I have privilege over may have the space to improvise, to burn the theater to the ground, and to build whatever they may atop the ash.

That's my journey, and along it I have stumbled, fallen, been imperfect. But if our relationship serves to teach us anything, it's that it's never too late to try and change, and it isn't about being perfect.

The beauty is that we endeavor to make it so.

Goodbye, Mr. Zawel.

ACCOUNTABILITY IN CASTE AND INTERSECTIONALITY

A white woman walked into a café and placed an order with a barista who was too busy reading the front page of a newspaper to hear her. The woman pulled down the newspaper to gain the attention of the barista, revealing the face of a young Black woman whose eyes and slouching shoulders told a story of sorrow.

"I would like a grande, iced, sugar-free, vanilla latte with soy milk, and a sprinkle of nutmeg," the woman said in a frustrated tone.

"I'm sorry, miss, I'll get that for you now," the barista replied as she placed the newspaper on the counter and began making the drink.

The barista returned a moment later with the woman's order and mustered a slight smile, despite the obvious sadness she was feeling. The woman walked away as an Asian man walked up and began to place an order with the barista. A moment later, the woman walked back to the counter and interrupted the man as he was placing his order.

"I asked for nutmeg, this doesn't have any nutmeg," the woman said as she positioned herself in front of the man who was ordering and placed her drink on the counter.

"Excuse me, I'm in the middle of ordering my dr—" the man began but was stopped by the woman in the middle of his sentence.

"This will just take a moment," the woman said.

"I'm sorry, miss. My mind was on too many things, I'll get that fixed for you right after I finish with this gentleman's order," the barista said.

"You expect me to wait for you to finish with him first? I have things to do!" the woman replied.

"I understand, miss. But I have to help him right now, if you just give me—" the barista began but was interrupted by the woman.

"I don't have time for this. Let me speak to the manager," the woman demanded.

"But, miss, if you just give me a—" The barista tried to appeal to the woman but was interrupted again.

"The manager! Now, please!" the woman replied.

The barista walked through a door behind the counter to speak with her manager about the situation.

"You shouldn't have asked to speak with her manager. It really was not that serious," the man at the counter said to the woman.

"I don't need a man to tell me what I should or shouldn't do," the woman responded.

A moment later, the manager, an older white man, approached the counter with a coffee in his hand.

"I ordered a—" the woman began but was abruptly interrupted by the manager.

"A grande, iced, sugar-free, vanilla latte with soy milk, and a sprinkle of nutmeg. I'm sorry about your order, ma'am, here you go," the manager said with a smile as he handed the woman her coffee.

"Thank you, at least someone understands good service here. It wasn't just that she simply got the order wrong, she was purposely ignoring me when I came in. I felt attacked," the woman replied.

"I'm sorry about that. She will be reprimanded. Why don't you take a free newspaper for your trouble," the manager said as he handed the woman the newspaper the barista had placed on the counter minutes before.

The woman took the newspaper from the manager and looked at the front page, which displayed a photo of a young Black man who looked eerily similar to the barista. The headline read OFFICER ACQUITTED IN DEATH OF TEEN BOY WALKING HOME FROM SCHOOL.

"It's a shame, the things racists do. I wish more people understood that Black Lives Matter," the woman said, then rolled the newspaper up and walked out the door, new coffee in hand.

The introduction to this essay is something I've seen happen all too often. It's the people who face oppression in their own ways, and because of that consider themselves good allies to other communities, and who are often the most dangerous to the communities to which they consider themselves allies. Because they are often the people who refuse to be held accountable or are too egotistical to try and grow.

Being oppressed doesn't absolve you from being privileged. This is an important concept that I believe everyone must sit with at some point, whether on a micro or a macro level. We can't strategize the destruction of any oppressive system without also knowing how we exist within or benefit from it. For example, as a Black man I should not be above reproach for how I might be upholding the oppression of others (or myself) simply because I also face oppression.

The term *intersectionality*, coined by Dr. Kimberlé Crenshaw in her paper "Demarginalizing the Intersection of Race and Sex: A Black Feminist Critique of Antidiscrimination Doctrine, Feminist Theory and Antiracist Politics," explores how the different identities we hold affect our lived experience.

Dr. Crenshaw defines it as "a lens, a prism, for seeing the way in which various forms of inequality often operate together and exacerbate each other. We tend to talk about race inequality as separate from inequality based on gender, class, sexuality, or immigrant status. What's often missing is how some people are subject to all of these, and the experience is not just the sum of its parts."

We live in a world built upon the idea that multiple things can't be true at the same time, when in fact, this is the opposite of reality. Dr. Crenshaw's work dissects and sheds light on the fact that we all have numerous overlapping experiences and identities. Understanding this work, seeing the world through an intersectional lens, better allows people to understand and navigate the complexities of the many forms of oppression people suffer under.

Understanding the framework of intersectionality and developing a lens based on it allows a person to see how someone may be facing certain types of oppression while also benefiting from certain types of privileges. A person can be both oppressed and privileged at the same time.

Take me for example. I am a cisgender heterosexual man, therefore I benefit from patriarchy, heteronormativity, and cisgender normativity. But I am also a Black person, a disabled person, and someone who still must navigate poverty in numerous ways, so I am oppressed by racism, ableism, and classism.

Intersectionality has been instrumental in helping me understand how groups such as Black women are systematically more oppressed than I am, and the importance of not only understanding why and how—but also using what privilege I do have to help make change. Black women are facing the toll of global anti-Black racism, same as I am, but unlike me they are also facing patriarchy, which I benefit from.

Additionally, America, like most nations and communities, operates under a caste system, a fact that was brought into mainstream consciousness by author Isabel Wilkerson in her 2020 book, *Caste*.

There are differing opinions about the levels of caste, in terms of who or what belongs where, but I've not seen any debate that in America's caste system, whiteness is at the top and Blackness is at the bottom based on historical and current contexts of amassed power and privilege. These ideas of intersectionality and caste in America are often best represented by the racial and gender wealth gaps, in which white men have accrued significantly more wealth than everyone else on average. While Black men and white women have far less wealth in comparison to white men, white women historically have amassed more wealth than Black men because of their proximity to white men and access to opportunity through whiteness. The median wealth of a single white man under thirty-five is $22,640, which is 3.5 times greater than that of a single white woman at $6,470. This number is 14.6 times greater than the $1,550 for a single Black man; both are greater than the $101 of Black women, and all three groups earn significantly more than trans Black women and men, who are often not even considered in analysis.

It's important to note that after the age of fifty-five, single Black women hold $40,760 in median wealth compared to single Black men with $27,100. But both are still significantly below white men and women, at roughly $400,000 and $216,000, respectively. Also, wage and wealth statistics don't include incarcerated populations, a fact that has major implications for metrics relating to Black men.

Caste and intersectionality also offer more context for the power and privilege dynamics that determine who is truly at the relative "top." As discussed, cisgender Black men are at the top of the patriarchal and white supremacist caste within the

Black community, and therefore they hold the most accountability and ability to make change in that subsection of the population. But in identifying communities from national and global vantage points, the only group that holds more power and privilege than white women is white men.

Reflecting again upon the racial and gender wealth gaps in America doesn't just give us an anecdote about white women making more money than members of the Black community, it tells a profound story. White women didn't truly enter the labor force until the 1900s in this country, and their number rose significantly during the 1930s and 1940s because of industrial and technological advancements as well as the demand created by World War II. Meanwhile, the entire Black community has been a part of the labor force since 1619, constituting the *sole unpaid labor force* of this country. Yet white women managed to outearn the Black community on average from the moment they entered the labor force three centuries later. Their unrivaled proximity to white men in the white supremacist, patriarchal system allowed them to propel themselves into economic prosperity faster than any other group.

This is why when discussing the dismantling of patriarchy and white supremacy we must view the experiences of marginalized groups through an intersectional lens and hold everyone accountable for the privileges they hold based on the oppression of others. That accountability is the only way actual change will occur.

ON PATRIARCHAL VIOLENCE

What he was able to offer beforehand was a trigger warning.

It took me a long time to figure out how I wanted to frame this entry, and more important, what I have to offer the conversation. Having spent a great deal of time not only researching and reading, but watching and living, I believe my best offering is perspective. The kind of perspective that comes from someone who has been both victim and abuser, in some instances without even realizing it.

I believe the first point I need to address in discussing patriarchal violence is my definition of "violence." I consider violence to be anything that may cause harm toward another person in any capacity. Meaning actions that affect a person's physical, mental, or emotional well-being can all be violent. Punching someone is an act of physical violence, as referring to someone by a slur is an act of emotional and mental violence. But ultimately, even if the violence is not physical, mental and emotional violence may also trigger physical harm.

This definition allows for my personal understanding that like most things, violence exists on a spectrum and may be perpetrated by anyone in a position of structural or systemic power. The concept of patriarchal violence speaks to the intersectional actions, systems, structures, policies, and beliefs that harm women, LGBTQ+ people, children, and other groups. As the Abolishing Patriarchal Violence Innovation Lab states, "PV is a global power structure and manifests on the systemic, institutional, interpersonal, and internalized level. It is rooted in interlocking systems of oppression."

Caste and intersectionality play a dual role in helping us understand patriarchal violence and how people may occupy roles as both victim and abuser.

White women hold a dual position in that way, both as recipients of systemic gender violence and as supporters of systemic racial violence, among others. White women are in a constant balancing act of upholding white supremacist systems and structures while also facing the oppressive violence of patriarchy. Patriarchal violence gives us the language and framing to best understand and navigate this kind of intersectionality.

The framing offered by patriarchal violence also considers the power dynamics and vulnerabilities in same-sex relationships and with children. To understand lesbian/bi/trans women survivors and gay/bi/trans men survivors, we must be able to examine the many ways violence may manifest outside of the heteronormative structure of male/female relationships. The lives and acts of LGBTQ+ people often defy gender, sex, and sexuality norms. To identify patterns of violence, it is essential to understand dominance, intimidation, and other behaviors.

Nuances of the LGBTQ+ community speak to another important aspect of dismantling patriarchal violence—understanding the lack of protection for those who face it. Like children, women have historically had few to no protections from violent acts committed against them. This situation is especially dangerous for those seeking help from the justice system and/or law enforcement, as police and other state agencies historically considered many acts to be personal or household problems that fell beyond the scope of criminal law until just a few decades ago. We should also take into account that over 80 percent of police officers in America are men and over 75 percent are white, many of them conditioned in the same white supremacist patriarchal structures as most of the country. The difference is that the rest of us aren't charged with the duty of protecting people who at best we don't understand, and at worst we may hate. This reality is at the root of disproportionate police brutality and criminality. It's also why many oppressed people live at the intersection of fear, anger, and disillusionment regarding law enforcement.

In learning more about patriarchal violence, I found this quote by Lydia Bates of the Southern Poverty Law Center deeply helpful. She speaks to the importance of understanding patriarchal violence and how using it as a framework can help protect marginalized lives that are often not considered in other frameworks of violence. "[Patriarchal violence] draws upon iterations of misogyny, racism, and homophobia across generations to contextualize and bring visibility to the on average thirty- to thirty-five-year lifespan of trans women of color in the Americas."

Domestic violence is often considered solely in terms of cisgender women's experiences with violence at the hands of men, but that perspective doesn't get to the root of the problem, which is the institution of patriarchal violence itself. Scholar, feminist, and author bell hooks often points out that if the abuse movement does not support all those who are abused, in many ways it's counterproductive and can't truly succeed.

Patriarchal violence can also be assessed through the experiences of children. Many of us were raised by parents whose ways of disciplining us—yelling, spanking, and verbal degradation—actually fell on the spectrum of patriarchal violence. I personally grew up in a neighborhood where most houses were solely headed by women, many of whom were Black. Many of their discipline practices were based on behaviors learned from and rooted in institutions such as chattel slavery. Making a child walk outside to get a switch is as much patriarchal violence as it is white supremacist conditioning. The idea that you have to violently break down a person or child in order to discipline them is pervasive within many cultures and communities. Many of our own sexist beliefs lead us to assume that women can't also commit acts of patriarchal violence because we don't believe them capable of said dominance and power.

Patriarchal violence may also exist even if an act of violence is not being committed. Parents who instill in their children, especially their sons, the belief that violence is an acceptable way to control social situations are not only being complicit in patriarchal violence but also upholding it. Teaching patriarchal violence to children may be as simple as saying "If they hit you, hit them back" or reinforcing sexist standards such as telling a brother he has to physically defend his sister. Even if the parents are not using violence, they may inspire children who will one day be adults to do so. The boy who was scolded for crying instead of fighting becomes the man who can address his emotional states only through violent rage.

IN DEFENSE OF BLACK WOMEN

BLACK WOMEN ARE NOT YOUR MULES

It wasn't enough for her to just be hated because of her womanhood, they made sure she was reviled for her Blackness at the same time.

"Let her do it, she's strong."

"Let her do that, too."

"Yeah, and that."

"What do you mean it's too much? I thought she was strong!"

I take a personal interest in many issues, and one of them is protecting and supporting Black women. When I was growing up, my mother often spoke of how important it is for Black people to protect one another: "If we don't have each other, who do we have? Who cares about Black people but Black people?" Both my mother and my grandmother leaned into that idea. The other Black children in the neighborhood could come to our house and get food; if a Black person was homeless, my mother and grandmother would find some old clothes to give them; and despite our family not having much for ourselves, if a Black person in the neighborhood needed help in any other way, they did their best to provide it.

But sadly, this was a light I didn't necessarily live in when I was younger. Largely because I didn't see Black men in my neighborhood carry themselves the same way my mother and grandmother did. The Black men in the neighborhood may have had each other's backs, but that solidarity rarely seemed to extend to Black women. In fact, I distinctly remember times men would catcall and disrespect my mother even as she would thoughtfully ask them to stop. In one instance, when I was likely about seven years old, a group of men followed my mother and me down the block as we were walking to the store. They were whistling and shouting things at her that make my fists clench as I think about them.

At one point my mother turned back and attempted to make a case for them to stop because she was with me: "I'm with my son, can't you respect that and leave me alone?" They didn't care. Eventually we reached the grocery store and stayed inside much longer than ever before, as my mother waited in the hope that the men weren't waiting outside for her. Fortunately, one of the store owners could tell something was wrong and walked us home.

While those types of men weren't the rule of the neighborhood, they also weren't the exception. I always knew I didn't want to be one of those men, but the reality is that when I was young, I didn't do much to combat them either.

I can think of far too many occasions when I chose to uphold toxic and violent behaviors by doing nothing about them. But the moments that haunt me constantly are the ones in which I did nothing to specifically protect Black women as they faced the wrath of anti-Black racism and patriarchal toxicity in front of me. Especially when that patriarchal toxicity was being perpetrated by other Black men. But there is one moment in which I let a Black woman feel unsupported or uncared for that is seared into my brain and wakes me up some nights in sweat.

When I was about fifteen years old, I played on a local amateur basketball team that was failing miserably. The team had a great deal of talent, but the coaching was disengaged and lacked overall effort. Identifying the need for a coaching change, a few parents went to the administrators of the league and had the head coach and his staff, all of whom were white men, fired. One of the administrators had a friend who played Division 1 college basketball who they thought might be open to filling the head coach position and hiring staff for the next season. This person accepted, and all of us were excited upon hearing that we would have not only a new head coach but one who had played Division 1 college basketball.

Months later, when training for the next season was set to begin, we were introduced to our new head coach, who ended up being a Black woman. Her name was Patricia Stephens, and she had played for one of the top basketball programs in the country and assembled a staff of coaches who were all men that also had played college basketball, though none had played Division 1, or for a program as impressive as hers. She was a very tall woman who likely made many toxic men feel inferior because of her stature alone, with a dark brown complexion and serious eyes that matched her demeanor.

From the very beginning it was obvious that Coach Stephens was not only more invested in our success than the prior coaching staff, but also far more knowledgeable and talented. She saw the full potential of our team and had devised plans for us to reach it, but most of the team refused to take her seriously because she was a woman. And more important, because she was unapologetic about it. Coach Stephens didn't begin her tenure trying to validate herself to us as a basketball mind. She knew that we needed her far more than she needed us, and most of the boys on the team didn't like that. Personally, I thought we had a great opportunity, especially because the alternative was a coaching staff of older white men who would constantly make racially charged comments. But it was obvious that most of my teammates had less of an issue with being led by problematic white men than they did with being led by a Black woman.

During Coach Stephens's tenure with the team, the players made her life hell. They refused to listen to her instructions in practice, became verbally disrespectful, and at times even played "jokes" on her, such as leaving unwrapped condoms all over the outside of her car.

But Coach Stephens kept coming to practice and trying to do her job. During the final practice before our season opening game, our best player simply refused to run any of the plays she was calling. She ran over to him and yelled, "*What is your damn problem?* I'm trying to help you all get to the next level." He looked at her and replied, "I'm not letting no bitch tell me how to play ball." Then he dropped the ball and walked off the court. Except for me and about three other players, the rest of the team left with him. Coach Stephens stared at her fellow coaches, who were both Black men, then stared at us remaining players in sheer disappointment. Then she walked out the gym.

That night I told my mother what had happened and she asked, "Well, when that happened and all of the other things happened, what did you do?"

I replied, "Nothing, because I—" My mother quickly interrupted me. "You didn't do anything because you were being a coward. It's easier to let a bunch of Black boys disrespect a Black woman just trying to do her job, trying to help your asses, than it is to step up and defend her. I'm not raising a Black man who doesn't defend Black women. All we do constantly is defend y'all. What about us? Look how you let them do her! Y'all aren't much different than the men around her who can't take no for an answer!"

My mother walked out the room and left me to mull over my cowardice.

That night I reflected on the things I had seen happen to my mother and what my teammates had done to Coach Stephens. I decided I was going to apologize to her and let the team know how wrong they had been. But when I got to practice the next day, I learned that Coach Stephens had quit and was being replaced by one of the Black men on her coaching staff, who hadn't defended her either. I seemed to be the only one who was unhappy about her leaving, so I tried to explain to my teammates what they had done, but none of them cared. In fact, I got into one argument with a teammate that turned into a fight.

I think about Coach Stephens often, as I never had the chance to apologize to her. But I decided I needed to grow and change, so that I wouldn't stand by idly as more Black women were left to face situations as my mother or Coach Stephens had while feeling that the Black men they so vehemently supported gave them nothing but trauma and disrespect in return.

As a Black man who hopes to support Black women as best as I can, I would be remiss if I didn't bring attention to a very specific way Black women are oppressed by those outside and inside our community. While all women face misogyny, as with most things, Black women face something far more insidious—misogynoir, a term coined by queer Black feminist Moya Bailey. Misogynoir is misogyny aimed at Black women where both gender and racial bias manifest at the same time.

Though the term was introduced less than two decades ago, Black women have been publicly speaking out against misogynoir for as long as Black women have been able to legally voice their opinions. Black women are often stereotyped by tropes such as sassy, angry, strong/durable, and hypersexual. These prevailing tropes create a lens through which many people see and interact with Black women. The term *misogynoir* provides language for contextualizing how all of this may be found in subtle and overt ways within society.

For example, because Black women have been historically stereotyped as "strong and durable," many healthcare professionals have given them less than adequate care. Black women are more than three times as likely as white women in the United States to have a maternal death. This trope, juxtaposed with that of the hypersexual Black woman, is also why accusations of sexual harassment or assault of Black women and girls are often ignored or not taken seriously.

The same hypersexual identity that is draped over Black women by anyone but themselves may be seen in how Black women's bodies are often regarded in society as inherently sexual objects. The treatment of Serena Williams by the mainstream media and stakeholders in international tennis provides a prime example. Serena's physique is what some would consider "voluptuous"; she is muscular and curved in ways that some of her high-profile counterparts are not. Because of this, there has been a great deal of conversation throughout her career about what she should and shouldn't wear, even when she was wearing the exact same attire as the white women she was playing against. Serena has also faced scrutiny for defending herself in instances where she feels she has been unfairly treated by a referee, causing people to weaponize the angry Black woman trope against her. The fact that these criticisms are not levied in the same way at her white counterparts shows that they are rooted not only in misogyny, but in misogynoir.

The #SayHerName movement also rose to prominence as a means of shedding light on how Black women have been erased from mainstream conversations about police violence and oppression. Black women's voices are too often stifled and their pain too often ignored by their supposed sisters in feminism and brothers in the Black community.

Misogynoir can also be found in how artist Megan Thee Stallion was treated by some Black men after the release of news and eventually a video in which she was shot in the foot by rapper Tory Lanez, a Black man. Megan was lambasted by many people, primarily Black men, on social media for going to the authorities over the shooting, even though she had originally tried to keep the incident out of the public eye. Some believed it was Megan's duty as a Black woman to protect Tory Lanez because of Black men's long history with overpolicing and murder by the American judicial system. In their misogynoir, they negated the reality that Black women such as Sandra Bland and Breonna Taylor also suffer under this system. They also ignored the fact that Tory Lanez was an abuser of a Black woman and had done clear harm to her in this instance, and there needed to be some form of protection and justice for that.

Understanding misogynoir allows us to consistently consider the intersection of oppression that Black women live at and face. This is especially important as so many of us attempt to rewrite the narrative that has cast Black women as deities in ways that often only serve other people: the all-knowing gods who supposedly feel no pain and are expected to answer our prayers whenever we need something. But who does a god turn to in need?

Society's religion does not actually praise Black women as much as it attempts to sacrifice them as mules and mammies.

Which is why one of my least favorite sentences in the English language is "Black women will save the world." Not because I don't believe Black women can do literally anything, but rather because I believe it's not their job to do it for anyone other than themselves. I don't believe Black women have some sort of genetic disposition to greatness, but this almost invincible or mythical lens is often the reason so many Black women don't receive the tenderness or protections they need and want. Rather, their strength and ability to succeed are self-fulfilling prophecies that come from the need to survive in spite of the forces that aim to destroy them.

I believe much of the wider narrative about Black women's ability to be strong is stereotyped in order to silence and gaslight them about how they are disenfranchised and exploited within white and Black communities.

Black women have always been asked to bear the brunt of the physical and emotional labor for a country that historically doesn't benefit them for doing so. Since being brought to the shores of this country, Black people have faced immeasurable oppression while fighting for their liberation, but Black women have also been forced to face oppression from those supposedly fighting on the same side they are. This can be seen in how many self-identified Democrats, especially white feminists, laud Michelle Obama now but were fairly quiet when she faced misogynoir from liberal media and talking heads just a dozen years ago.

One particular instance comes to mind: when *The New Yorker* released a cover on which Michelle Obama and Barack Obama were depicted as threatening Black radicals, with Michelle's hair in an afro and both her and Barack armed with AK-47 assault rifles and doing what many have called "a terrorist fist bump." While the cover drew the ire of many people in Black and brown communities, there was an especially telling silence from white liberals, including feminists. It was Black women who insulated and did their best to support Michelle Obama during that period. Michelle spent years being scrutinized about her hair, her physique, her intellect, and her interests in ways that almost always blatantly oozed misogynoir. But still, she was largely only supported by Black feminist institutions.

Eight years later, Michelle became a darling of both liberal media and white feminists in the wake of Donald Trump's presidential victory over Hillary Clinton. The Democrats, and mainstream feminists, needed a beacon and face to combat white supremacy. If history proved nothing else, it was that Black women had always been the most capable for the job. But in all those instances, everyone else benefits, while only Black women pay the costs.

There is a through line from the treatment of Black women during the women's suffrage movement to the silence about the misogynoir Michelle Obama faced. While white women received the glory and acclaim in the fight for women's rights over a century ago, it was actually Black women such as Sojourner Truth who were the backbone of the movement. All while being literally spat on by the white women who were supposed to be their sisters.

Black women have not only risen to the occasion of saving themselves and those around them, but they've done so while bolstering themselves within systems that were designed for them to fail. One of these systems is higher education, in which Black women have become the most accomplished group in America. But as was the case with Michelle Obama, when

Black women are in positions of power, privilege, and access, they aren't praised for their ingenuity or strength. Instead they are too often demonized and met with vitriol from all those whom they historically, and currently, work to liberate.

America wants Black women to put on a cape and constantly save the rest of us, without caring that the very people they are saving are their kryptonite. Black women saving the day is not sustainable, but more important, it's not fair. If there is a road to a better, stronger, and more equitable democracy and society, it can't be made on the backs of Black women. Rather, we will know it's possible when Black women feel the weight on their backs lifted.

DEAR OLUWATOYIN

From reading about her, he understood that many who knew her referred to Oluwatoyin as "Toyin," but he didn't know her. He never had the chance to ask her how she would prefer he refer to her, and he wanted to be as respectful of every aspect of her as he could, especially of her name. Because often, that is all we have.

Oluwatoyin,

Had we been near each other on a sidewalk or in a café, we would not have known each other. I would not have known if you changed your hairstyle recently. You wouldn't have been surprised to see me wearing glasses, which I rarely do in public. We would have been strangers, and yet, you were my younger sister.

We are all children lying under the same quilt, working the same field, beads of sweat dripping down our brows from toiling under the same sun. I was your brother and you were my sister.

Part of the magic of being Black is that we are all bound by both the jubilee and the harrowing journey. In other words, I suppose we are never actually strangers.

I imagine the gray hairs in my beard and the slouching of my shoulders would have been familiar to you. As the likely resolve and *weariness in your eyes would have been familiar to me. The plight of the Black American.*

We would have merely been two Black people momentarily sharing space, though that has always been enough to change the world.

It's likely that we wouldn't have spoken to each other, because words aren't always needed. There is a look between Black people; it happens quickly, and others never catch it. It's in the eyes, the smile, the head nod. It says, "Good luck and be safe."

A simple look exchanged between us, a generational understanding of well wishes on the road ahead. Wherever it may lead.

But there was no street, no café, no well wishes.

I first learned about your death through an image my friend posted on social media. It was a Photoshop design of you surrounded by flowers. Your head was tilted to the side with your chin gently rested upon your hands. The image was beautiful, yet the only thing I thought when I saw it was "Not another one. She looks so young."

I've always found it especially heartbreaking and unnatural to watch the old bury the young. To eulogize someone and instead of reflecting on a life lived, be left pondering a life that could have been.

Posts like the one that introduced me to you have become a staple for a community trying to find ways to honor those who have been stolen from us. I feel nauseous every time I see one.

But it wasn't queasiness I felt in the pit of my stomach while reading your story, it was my heart. After learning about your fate I was numb, and then as I sat alone in my living room, I thought deeply on the tragedy that had befallen you and I became inconsolable.

I don't cry much anymore when I learn of someone's death, not because I'm against shedding tears, but rather because I don't have many left. I spent so much time crying for the very people you were protesting for, and those who we lost long before them.

But I found tears for you, sister, and once I did, I couldn't unfind them.

You were only nineteen. Nineteen. I couldn't help but think about how much life I had lived since I was that age, the things I had felt, the places I had seen. You were robbed, and what made it worse, it was by the same people you were fighting for.

One of us, one of ours. A Black man. I've struggled with this more than I can articulate. "Monolithic" will never describe the array of Blackness, but I can't make heads or tails of this villainy.

He came to you in your time of need, and you trusted him. We should be able to trust those we toil in the sun with, we should be able to trust those next to us in the field, we should be able to trust the other children under the quilt.

As your eyes were fixated on God and liberty, his were infatuated with Satan and shackles.

But there you were, fighting for us, all while being ignored by us.

Thousands of people saw your call for help, hoped for you, dreamt for your safety, but hands were not offered. We didn't serve you as you had served us, we left you to fight for your life alone.

Some said watching you out there was like "magic." You were in fact a very gifted orator with a brave soul, but I can't accept or reinforce the idea that watching Black people fight for their freedom is magical or mythical. It does a disservice to our flesh, our bones, and our mortality.

When you needed us most, we weren't there for you. There is nothing magical about that. There is only a nineteen-year-old Black woman left to be preyed upon and stolen from a world she fought so courageously to fix.

We didn't protect you from ourselves, Oluwatoyin. We failed to make sure that you grew old, younger sister.

In some ways, Black people never get to be young, not truly. Shortly after our first steps, we are gifted with the weight of the world, while white children receive the deeds to the land that's soaked in our blood.

This is the same curse that placed you on the front lines of a fight I wish was left to those of us who have felt the warmth of a few more summers.

The older I get, the more I both admire and worry about the courage and expectations of young people. Your generation is particularly compelling in that way.

I'm of the generation that focuses on representation as opposed to liberation. A group that overly leaned into Obama's popularization of hope, which is another word for dream. While both are important, neither guarantees action.

Your generation does more than hope—it demands. There is an expectation of freedom, opportunity, and liberation. I watched a video of you speaking in which you began by saying "Black lives matter," then quickly followed with "Black trans lives matter"; you paused for a second and repeated yourself slowly, "Trans lives matter."

You weren't asking a question, or sharing a concept, you were making a demand. A proclamation. If there is a Black life in any shape or form, you were fighting to make sure it mattered.

This beautifully unwavering humanity is at the core of your generation. Truth seems to be the only thing worth speaking to power, and if power will not listen, you all are ready to burn whatever is necessary until it does.

I've stood proud, smiling, and basking in the glow of the embers watching you all battle beside me. But the issue with fire is that it often engulfs not only what it was meant to destroy, but also those who lit it.

The danger of fighting for liberation is that you will likely never see it. The danger of being in this fight so young is that you may never see anything. There should be an age limit on martyrdom.

When I think of young Black people like you, I'm often reminded of a verse from the song "To Be Young, Gifted and Black" by Nina Simone:

*We must begin to tell our young
There's a world waiting for you
Yours is the quest that's just begun*

I recently found myself crying in the shower while it played in the background. Those specific lyrics have always stood out to me, but this time they reminded me of you.

Tragedy came knocking at your door, and someone, anyone, should have made sure you didn't have to answer. Made sure you could experience a quest that was just beginning. My sorrow nearly washed me away that day, but your courage and fire demanded that I honor you instead.

But how do I honor the sister I never knew? How do I lay flowers of praise at your feet as you deserve, when I'm not sure what kind of praise you would want? As I combed through photos and videos of you, there were many words in my heart, but my pen never seemed to do them justice. Words such as "courageous," "graceful," and "poised." It's a paradox really, the same words used to uplift Black women are also used as excuses not to support them.

There were other words as well, words that carry the water of your untimely demise. Words such as "unfair" and "young." Though there is never an appropriate age to have one's life taken.

For many, honoring you and other Black women has manifested in the way of saying your names. Making sure the world knows you were here, you were important, and you were loved. My soul told me that my mission is to make sure no one ever forgets your name.

Which is why I decided to write this letter to you. As a way of holding you in the light of glory, because I refuse to merely use your name and image with a hashtag and move on.

May my words serve as penance, an endeavor to eulogize and apologize to the countless Black women, like yourself, who were let down and betrayed by our community.

Maybe in some other place, better than this one, we actually spent time together. I got to know you, not just the you that lives in others' memories, but the real you. What you hoped for, what you feared, what your favorite movie was, what your favorite foods were. I find myself wondering what you read, what you watched, what experiences led you to become the brilliantly intersectional activist I've seen in videos.

But in this life we didn't meet, and you didn't need my guidance, you needed refuge. I am so very sorry.

You're gone now, and I can't do anything about it, but I can offer you this: Your flame is eternal here. I will carry your name with me wherever I may go, and the names of everyone you fought for.

We will meet one day, in a place far better than this, but until then your fire will help me continue to melt down the shackles that your spirit was too large for. I will repurpose what is left for the shield and sword that will protect our other sisters.

This I promise you.

Goodbye, my young, gifted, and Black sister.

Your brother,
Fred

BLACK BODY POLITICS

She had spent her life being told her body was too much, that it wasn't right. Now her body was perfect, it was her skin that wasn't right.

My grandmother's body was stolen,
Divine
to work lands that were not theirs,
my wife's body was stolen,
Bountiful
to care for children from another womb,
my mother's body was stolen,
Graceful
to help quench his thirst,
my sister's body was stolen,
Black
to be told that it was too much,
my daughter's body will not be stolen,
Free
to celebrate what you told her you despise.

MY MOTHER'S SON

But Mom, I don't know how to
be both the best and worst parts
of all of them.

I am not my mother's drawing,
merely my mother's son.
Repurposed pieces of what was left,
by those who left.
A figment of imagination,
of a woman who is trying,
to figure out what a man should be.
I am not my mother's painting,
but I am "just like" the father I've never met.
Who is just like the father she only met once.
Who is just like the men I thought I wasn't
supposed to be until "why can't you be more like."
An inferno started by a flame,
lit with a dusty match,
from an old coat no one wore.
Sculpture made of sand,
at the beach in a typhoon.

I am not my mother's song,
but rather the silence returned,
when I hear I am not who she raised
me
to be.

NOTES FROM A KING

We all know what it's like to be told that there is not a place for you to be featured. Yet you are young, gifted and Black. We know what it's like to be told to say there's not a screen for you to be featured on, a stage for you to be featured on. We know what it's like to be a tail and not the head. We know what it's like to be beneath and not above. That is what we went to work with every day because we knew . . . that we had something special that we wanted to give the world. That we could be full human beings in the roles that we were playing. That we could create a world that exemplified a world that we wanted to see.

—Chadwick Boseman

Dear Chadwick,

I began writing this letter to you on the night I found out you were gone. A short while after I was finally able to lift myself from the floor, having been brought to it by the gravity of you leaving this world. I'll never forget that moment, Chadwick. As I received the devastating news, I thought of your eyes, and then I thought of

*photos of you and your wife, Simone, and how similar your eyes
are. I remember meeting her in Los Angeles at an event and both of
us gushing over how excited we were for* Black Panther *to release.
After our conversation I remember my friend Travis saying, "She
seemed really nice. That says a lot about Chadwick." He was right,
she was very nice. But more than nice, she seemed kind. Which is
how your eyes were similar, you both have such kind eyes.*

*After thinking about your eyes for some time, I thought about
many other eyes, some I've seen, and some I've not. They belong to
our people, this beautiful Black family that must constantly be reminded of its mortality. Constantly reminded of how fleeting* here
and now *are for us.*

*My dungeon floods with tears thinking about how early our
heroes become ancestors, often before we can give them the flowers
they deserve. For what you accomplished in your time with us and
for us, gardens should be grown in your honor, my dear brother. You
didn't just play the roles of heroes; you took on the task of opening the
mind and widening the imagination to Black futures.*

*I nearly drowned in my tears that night. But I don't know that
they were tears for my own grief, as much as they were tears for a
world that was now far less complete without you in it. Tears for
a family that has already been through so much—too much. It was
never lost on me what you meant to the world, even if the world
didn't always realize it at the time.*

*I've spent a lifetime holding so many emotions for our people—
anger, disappointment, fear, and so much more. But I can't recall
feeling more heartbroken for us than the night you were called home.*

Why is time a luxury that never seems to be afforded to Black people? Why must the mortality of our heroes be so ever-fleeting? How much more loss can live in our collective body?

Since that night, many words have poured out of me onto these pages, yet I've never been able to fully convey what it is that I've wanted to say to you until now. It never felt right—never felt like enough. At first I thought it was because I refused to truly accept that you were gone, which is why for months I couldn't bring myself to watch your award-winning performance in Ma Rainey's Black Bottom. *I guess I wanted something to hold on to, an ellipsis rather than a period. But eventually I came to terms with the fact that I couldn't continue to avoid the film or the truth. When I finally mustered up the emotional courage to watch it, I realized what had been missing from my letter to you was honesty. I wasn't saying everything I really felt.*

I believe anyone can be trained in the skills it takes to create art, but only those bold enough to leave honest pieces of themselves in their art will create something special. Which is why your performances were exactly that—special. But that final performance of yours as Levee took it to another level. You weren't merely acting with honesty. You were existing unapologetically within the role. In those moments of Levee's tears, fury, frustration, and weariness, we weren't getting simply parts of you—we were getting you. The essence of who you were beyond the lights seemed to drape itself around that character, creating something historic and unprecedented. Something I had only seen in moments when people I'm closest to felt safe enough to open a window to the deepest and most profound parts of themselves.

What a performance.

God ain't never listened to no nigger's prayers. God take a nigger's prayers and throw them in the garbage. God don't pay niggers no mind. In fact, God hate niggers! Hate them with all the fury in his heart.

I felt myself shaken in awe when I heard you deliver those lines. There was an emotion that felt familiar, something I knew well. Those lines were delivered with the emotion of a man who sounded as if he was tired of being tired. I can't say whether when you filmed the role you were tired as Levee was tired, but I can say you understood what Levee was feeling. Something only a man who had spent his entire career creating space to show us how much he loved us could understand.

There is a toll that comes with spending so much of your time writing love letters to people through your art. People see you as a hero, but few see that you are still a human. I have to wonder whether in that final performance we saw some of that toll. Possibly some of the mortality of a man who had given so much love to the public while fighting a war in private.

It was the honesty in your eyes while playing Levee and potentially letting us truly see you that reminded me why I wanted to write to you. After your passing there was a sea of thanks and condolences that flooded the internet in reflection of your work and your gracious time with us. People discovered stories about you visiting children suffering with cancer in the hospital and supporting countless non-profit organizations, all while secretly suffering from cancer yourself. The mythos and lore of Chadwick Boseman only grew in the days following the news of your home going.

Which is why I thought it was important to do more than thank you. We always thank people once they're gone, but do we ever let them know that we saw them?

I was reading Toni Morrison's Beloved *recently and when Sethe said, "Love is or it ain't. Thin love ain't love at all," I immediately thought about watching as Simone had accepted an award a few weeks earlier on your behalf. She spoke of how appreciative you would be, but made sure that much of her time was spent speaking to the cancer that stole you from her. She was direct and knowledgeable about how colon cancer disproportionately affects Black men, and why we should be screened consistently. She has a love for us not unlike your own. Thick love—nothing close to thin.*

But, while I appreciated her attempt to help save the lives of someone else's husband, father, or brother, I couldn't help but consider whether she was being gracious with herself. Whether something was being sacrificed within the individual for the greater collective. Maybe her courage in that moment was cathartic for her, I can't say. But I hope her well is being poured into, and not simply drawn from.

Do the people with kind eyes and selfless hearts ever get to be selfish with their pain?

I've messaged her a few times to let her know my household is happy to support her if ever she needs something. I hope many others are doing the same.

When she posts photos of you it reminds me of Porsche, my

fiancée, and how often our partners are forced to share us with the world. A world that is not always as kind as the world we are trying to build. There are so few conversations about the toll on our partners for loving us in this world. For loving those of us who have endeavored to show others a thick love—a love that is. But what if love isn't a matter of is or ain't? What if there should be room to breathe in between?

I suppose the honesty I mentioned leaning into is the fact that there was a long period after your passing that I had to take that breath. My love didn't adhere to the binary of is or ain't, it was somewhere else, somewhere lying in a bed next to my disappointment in us. Before you passed, I vividly remember you posted a video for an initiative called Operation 42. It was an effort meant to raise awareness about donating medical equipment to hospitals supporting the Black community during Covid-19. It seemed like a wonderful effort, but as did others, I also noticed you had become much slimmer than I had ever seen you. I was concerned, especially because I had seen people lose that amount of weight before. People I had seen in far too many hospices that I had spent far too much time in. I showed Porsche the video, and she was worried as well. I went to your IMDb page to see if you might be preparing for a role, but nothing seemed aligned with the weight loss. Whatever you had been private about was likely meant to stay private.

I'm not one to read comments on social media, so I hadn't seen what people were saying in response to your weight loss. But I eventually found out through an article that you had removed the post about Operation 42, along with many others, because of the disgust-

ing comments and jokes about your appearance on your social media accounts. Comments from the very people you had written so many love letters to. The people you had made such a kind and loving space for. I was enraged upon learning about how you were being treated. How could they be so cruel? No one deserved it, but especially not you. I would be remiss if I didn't tell you that. Tell you how sorry I am that you had to endure that.

It was many of those same people who offered condolences and kind words after your passing. That's around the same time that my love began to fall back on the binary and teetered toward thin. There was one night I was a few glasses away from finishing an entire bottle and I was thinking about all the death and loss of 2020, and then I thought of your kind eyes and how I felt so many people didn't deserve to see them. I fell asleep shortly after the bottle was done with me.

The next morning, I woke up and saw a post on my timeline that had photos of you in some of your most iconic roles. The caption read: "He was someone who always knew the assignment." I stared at that post for a long time and thought about it all day. You were exactly what we needed when we needed it most, someone that all of us, especially our children, can hold on to and live up to. Most of my on- and off-screen heroes growing up were largely manifestations of white colonial patriarchy. I wanted to be Shaft, I wanted to be Jim Brown, I wanted to be my uncles. They were all I had in a world where so many Black men are stolen from us and the most popular, dynamic, and seemingly pure-hearted heroes only come in various shades of white. These were the few Black men I saw being revered, wise, strong, and unapologetic, yet in reality they were barely any of those things.

I thought about how your artistry helped us imagine what a version of Black masculinity not steeped in toxic patriarchal ideologies looks like. I wonder how I might have been different had I grown up with your portrayal of Black Panther, a king whose most endearing quality is the way he actively tries to make sure he isn't taking space from queens but rather creating it. In playing the first major Black superhero, you reminded all of us who and what we were before the chains, before the ships, before the fields, and before the disease that is white patriarchy. You reminded me that being a hero to my future sons and the boys in my life starts with doing my part in making sure they become men who don't exist as people who draw their power from the oppression of women.

The weight of your performance led me into a deep sleep where you came to me in a dream. We were sitting somewhere beautiful, though I can't remember what it looked like. You said something profound, though I can't remember what your words were. But somehow, neither of those things mattered when I woke up, what mattered was how I felt. I understood that the things people had said about you weren't about you, they were about themselves. Their own self-hate and agony. They were people who needed thick love the most.

Truly having a love that is sometimes means loving people even when they can't reciprocate it, even when their love isn't.

I believe that was your assignment, and maybe it's Simone's, maybe it's Porsche's. To show our family how thick a love can be. In *turn, that reminds all of us how we might learn to love ourselves more. Honestly, I wasn't ready to love like that before. My love was swayable, even conditional, but I'm ready for it now. I'd like to continue your assignment if you'll have me.*

    Until we meet again, brother,
    Fred

P.S. I told my grandmother she would see you around. She'll help look after you if you ever need anything. Unless it's a meal. She adds smoked neck bones to almost everything and I remember you saying something in passing about being vegetarian. Peace and love.

WHAT DOES A BLACK PERSON OWE THIS COUNTRY?

He watched another boy who looked like the boy he once looked like be gunned down by those claiming to protect and serve him. A boy who, even if he had lived, might not have had health insurance for the treatment, because his parents couldn't afford to pay for their education in a country they built for free, one where most of the people who are hungry and houseless look like the boy and his parents. Why do boys who look like me and their family stay here if they don't have to?

2019

Last year marked my thirtieth year on this earth, which was a welcome surprise, as I was almost sure my mother, like her mother before her, would have to bury her eldest son. But against all odds, named and unnamed, I am still here.

Like most Black people in America, consciously or not, I consider my mortality almost daily. This doesn't come from some misguided infatuation with death, it comes from the understanding of white supremacy's infatuation with Black bodies.

In America, a Black child isn't afforded the luxury of blissful ignorance, not when measured against survival. Which is why when I was merely ten years old, my mother knew she had to teach me about the atrocities that had befallen our people. Atrocities such as the gruesome murder of Emmett Till. This is the weight that Black children bear.

I had to learn about the traps and land mines hidden all around us, always ready to destroy Black lives. In the case of fourteen-year-old Emmett Till, the land mine was a white woman's tears, as they so often are.

The first time my mother forced me to look at the photo of Emmett's lifeless body in his casket, I tried my best to turn away. "I'm sorry! But you have to look, you have to know!" my mother yelled as she grabbed my arm and turned me toward the photo.

It's a familiar moment to many Black people. The moment a Black parent has to make sure their child knows the world hates them, in hope that knowledge helps keep them alive.

The image of Emmett's brutally disfigured face has haunted me ever since—as my mother intended.

The more I learned about the barbarity Black people have faced, the more it became abundantly clear to me that for us, life is a scarce commodity. Which is why even though I don't celebrate most things, I make it a point to celebrate birthdays.

In a land where so much of our time is stolen, I believe we should laud what is still ours. A birthday does just that. Even if we don't celebrate for ourselves, it's our duty to lift the memories of those who are gone. Sandra Bland, Trayvon Martin, and

Tamir Rice, and all of our brothers and sisters who were robbed of their time.

My grandmother had her time stolen as well, though not in the same sense as those I just previously named. As it does with most Black people, white supremacy took her slowly. Rather than by bullets and choke holds, she was killed by poverty and a lack of resources. It's a story I've seen more times than I care to tell, an unfair life that deserved more living.

Like that of so many of us, her time here was mostly spent looking out the window dreaming of things she would never have. Dreams filled with writing, traveling, and other things that were out of reach for a single Black mother raising children in the projects. But they were dreams that she didn't give up. Instead, she deferred them to her grandson.

When I was a boy, my grandmother had an old globe. Sometimes the two of us would spin it and choose a random place we were going to visit together. Ghana, Egypt, Italy, anyplace that stretched our imaginations enough to forget that neither of us had ever been on an airplane and we were too poor to visit.

I was a wonderfully innocent child who dared to believe anything was possible if my mother or grandmother told me it was. What I wouldn't do to have that back.

The older I became, the more I understood my family's situation, and how unlikely us visiting any of those distant places was. But somehow, the more I settled into poverty, the more my grandmother dreamt.

"What's the first thing you want to eat when we get to Italy?" she would ask as we stood in line at the local food pantry along with everyone else in need. We played this game for years, until there was no time left to play it.

My grandmother would never visit Italy, in fact, she would never travel further than a few trips to the Carolinas. She battled breast cancer twice, not telling anyone that she had it the first time. The second time she didn't have an option, it was a fight she couldn't win.

As my grandmother lay on a hospice bed, preparing to end a life that was far less than she deserved, she held my hand and said, "Go see everything." The firmness of her grasp and the look in her tired eyes let me know it wasn't an ask, it was an instruction. So I promised her I would.

Thelma Ford passed three days later, but her dreams live on.

While I certainly didn't have a blueprint for doing so, I created a path that eventually allowed me to live our dreams. Like the paths of many Black people, mine has been paved with trauma and survivor's remorse. But again, I am still here.

Over the years I've visited places and had experiences that even my grandmother hadn't dreamt of, but I'm sure she is guiding.

Along my travels I was guided to Porsche. A woman who shares my thirst for freedom, adventure, and the belief that America's promise of liberty is one made to a chosen few. It was on these foundational values that we built a relationship and will soon build a marriage.

One could say ours is a love that exists at the intersection of liberation and reclaiming time. A love that, like all things that matter, is a constant work in progress.

While we come from completely different worlds, our stories are draped in similar American trauma. Which is why we have an unsaid understanding that we will leave this country at our backs as swiftly and often as possible.

It is the need to escape that finds us on a plane at random moments throughout the year. January is the only time of the year that our travel is rooted in tradition. Each year we take a trip for our birthdays, which are three days apart. In 2019, we decided to travel through parts of Europe.

The heaviness of America undermines any true celebrations of Black lives, so we leave. It's a trip I'm always excited to take, my own personal way of telling America I refuse to let it own my time. But this year I didn't just want to leave; it wouldn't be an exaggeration to say my very life depended upon it.

The older I get, the more I learn that there are moments that simply become forgotten anecdotes over time. Laughs you no longer remember having and tears you no longer remember shedding. But there are some moments that stay with a person forever, shaping the very nature of who you are at a molecular level—for good or bad.

My 2019 was a string of dreadful moments that I will never forget.

As the year came to a close, I was at an inflection point in my life. Which is a nice way of saying I had no idea what I was going to do next. I had just left my job as a marketing executive at a non-profit because of racism and was reeling from my experience.

I hadn't planned on working for that organization, or for anyone for that matter; I wanted to continue building my own agency. But they sold me on the idea that I could do more good in the world by combining my marketing talent, influence, and connections with their resources. We were supposed to make a difference.

As I said before, white supremacy has traps and land mines everywhere. In some cases, they are disguised as friends, or the more recent buzzword "allies."

I was an award-winning marketer with name recognition and numerous high-profile campaigns under my belt. But in spite of all of that, I was still young, and most important—Black. Which in their minds meant I was nothing, and they made sure I knew it.

Not even a token, I was treated as an ornament of sorts. Something to be displayed when the season was deemed appropriate and discarded as the weather changed. My days were filled with gaslighting, overt racism, and anxiety attacks. I didn't fall apart, I was pulled at the seams.

My time there amounted to one of those years you'd happily stumble out of in one piece, yet you find yourself crawling and gasping for air. Barely alive.

I took a leave of absence in December because the stress of the job was causing my multiple sclerosis to flare up. Then, with the encouragement of my fiancée, I decided to leave in January. It was a week before our trip.

I was afraid to leave, but it was the only way of stopping the further erosion of my mental and physical health. Luckily I was still doing some consulting and had recently signed a deal for my first book. It was enough to keep me afloat.

I decided to use the time away to plan my next steps and quickly put back some of the pieces that the year had knocked out of place. As is the case in most Black lives, there was no time to heal, no time to be broken.

Our vacation wasn't a celebration, but rather a triage.

We started the trip in Amsterdam because we got a good deal. I wasn't very enthused by the idea of trying to reflect and mend in a city most widely known for its brothels and bachelor parties. But I tend to find exactly what I need in places I never expect.

We booked a room about a ten-minute drive from the city center, an attempt to avoid exchanging the madness from our city for the madness in another. After arriving at our hotel, we decided to walk around and take in the area.

I have a love for places that are quaint and serene, likely because where I grew up was anything but. The types of places where a countryside bike ride is a person's daily commute, there's always a faint smell of baked goods in the air, and any turn may lead you to a pond where you can skip rocks. I always thought it was a fantasy reserved for romantic films and Nicholas Sparks novels.

The further I get away from where I grew up, the more I realize that it's not a fantasy, at least not for some. A chosen few who get to live while the rest of us are left dreaming. The benefits of whiteness.

Within minutes, Amsterdam felt like those fantasies. It was one of the most whimsically beautiful places I'd ever been. A picturesque world of canals, classic-looking bikes, and audacious architecture.

I so desperately wanted to let my guard down and enjoy my surroundings, but when you're Black, all beautiful things must be side-eyed and measured beyond their surface.

But as we spent our days there visiting shops, eating at cafés, and drinking at bars, something happened that I had only experienced one other time in my life. Nothing. I didn't experience anything negative or racially charged.

There was no one following me through shops to make sure I wasn't stealing, no one expecting my fair-skinned, biracial fiancée to be the one to pay for our meal, women didn't hold their purses closer as I walked by. For me, a Black man from America, this was anything but my normal daily experience.

There were people who seemed to turn their noses up at us, but they were doing the same with other tourists. I didn't mind that at all; everyone has a right to despise Americans. Though I do wish Black Americans were not associated with the evils of our country.

I wanted so badly to believe in Amsterdam, but can a Black person ever truly believe in any white place run by white people? Not a belief that racism didn't happen there, no such utopia exists. But rather a belief that, even if rare, there could be places and moments where I felt safe.

On our last day in the city, three particular interactions not only solidified Amsterdam as a better home than America, but also helped me imagine my own future. A future fit for a dreamer.

As we continued to get lost in the splendor of the city, we found ourselves visiting a small café called Cereal & Chill. The name doesn't leave much mystery, the café obviously served cereal. I was weary of the "chill" part as the phrasing is typically Black vernacular and its frequent appropriation made me think we were on the road to my first negative experience in this city.

When we arrived, I was pleasantly surprised. Not only was the café staffed by Black employees, but I quickly learned it was also Black-owned. There was classic hip-hop playing, nineties memorabilia strewn about, and vibrant photos of Black celebrities on the walls. It gave me a sense of security one could find in one's bedroom as a child.

I ended up making conversation with one of the owners, a German-born Black man who had immigrated to Amsterdam. We talked about everything from places we should visit next to the racial disparities in America versus Amsterdam. It was a quick conversation, but some of the best ones are, especially when they're honest.

He gave me an unbiased opinion of being Black in Amsterdam: "It's not perfect. But it doesn't hate Black people as much as America does." It was a truth that so few can understand.

White supremacy has always been a global issue, but America perfected it.

While Porsche and I both wished that sugary cereals were adequate sustenance, we had to find something else to eat when we left the café. There was a restaurant with good reviews nearby, so we headed there. As we walked in, a Black man was leaving with a friend and immediately stopped when he saw us.

He stared at me for a moment. "Fred?" he asked. I had no idea who this man was or what he could have wanted with me.

"Fred Joseph?" he continued. I immediately stepped in front of Porsche, expecting the worst. "Why here? Why now?" I thought.

"Yeah, that's me. Is there an issue?" I responded as I began to look around for anything I could quickly use to defend myself. The weight of a Black man's appropriate paranoia.

"No, no, I'm sorry! There is no issue. I follow you on Instagram and I love what you do. I love the things you talk about," he responded. Porsche and I looked at each other in surprise. She, too, had been expecting the worst.

My guard went down and I apologized for my disposition. He understood, especially because my social media posts often focus on being honest about my experiences with racism in America. We talked for a few minutes before he left; he was a very nice person and gave us some suggestions on what to do during a future trip to Amsterdam. It was nothing short of a life-changing moment.

For years I'd given my most transparent self on any platform where people could hear me, hoping that doing so would make some sort of change. But I had no idea anyone was actually listening, especially not in other parts of the world.

We sat down and before I could say a word Porsche looked at me and said, "I'm not surprised. People hear you." I had never seen myself as someone who could connect with people around the globe. Seeing this ability opened up a world of possibilities for the future.

Later that day we went back to our hotel to get some rest before dinner. Porsche decided to take a nap, but I stayed up, I needed to reflect.

I had been to many places that I wished my grandmother had seen, places I wanted to bring my mother to, but Amsterdam was different. It wasn't just a place to visit, it was a vision of what home should feel like. A place where Black people seemingly have more time.

We decided to have dinner at a restaurant that converted from a café where we'd had brunch earlier. There was nothing special about the food, but it was within walking distance, and the staff had been pleasant.

As we were leaving the hotel room, I went to turn off the television and saw the news was covering the articles of impeachment that had been presented against Donald Trump. A reminder of what was in store for us once we got home.

When we walked into the restaurant, we were immediately taken by how friendly everyone was, and the neo-soul playlist that filled the room with the sounds of artists such as Raphael Saadiq and Jill Scott. If I didn't know any better, I would have thought I was in one of my favorite New York City lounges.

The food was nearly as good as the music and provided the perfect end to what had been a wonderful few days before we headed to our next destination.

While we very much appreciated the music and the entire ambience that night, it was something I noticed throughout our time in Amsterdam. Outside of the cereal shop, we had also heard "Black music" in various places that didn't have Black people. Furthermore, it was never especially popular Black music. These were songs that, even in America, most white people didn't listen to.

I decided to ask our server about it. My question seemed to surprise her as much as her answer surprised me.

"I don't know. We listen to many types of things here, but there is a special appreciation for Black musicians speaking positively about the Black community. I think for white people in America, that doesn't exist as much," she said.

Her response not only answered my question in that moment but answered a broader question about my time in Amsterdam. Why was I treated differently here than I was in America? Her response made the answer simple: some places invest in appreciating humanity instead of investing in taking it away.

Some places may actually appreciate my Blackness, even if just some of the time. The thought was so foreign to me, it was nearly frightening.

We talked for a few more minutes as she told us more about Amsterdam, and we told her about what we did for a living and why we travel for our birthdays.

She then asked whether she could pose a question to me. I of course obliged. She prefaced her question with a starting point to show that she had thoughtfully assessed what she was about to ask. "Your country elected a white supremacist as president, you don't have basic human rights such as healthcare, you also have to deal with the dangerous police and fear for your lives nearly every day. Is this all true?"

"Yes," I responded.

She then took a deep breath, as if she was pondering whether she should ask the question. I gave her a look affirming she should continue. "Well, why don't you leave?" she asked.

I immediately thought of my grandmother and all of the people who had struggled because of the systems of white supremacy in America. All of the people who had dreamt of leaving, even for a moment, but never could. I told her that I disliked her question and it was steeped in privilege.

She looked at us both for a second and then said, "I'm sorry, I didn't mean to offend you, but I think you misunderstood my question. I'm not asking why your entire community doesn't leave. Leaving is very difficult, and it costs a great deal. What I'm asking is why the two of you don't leave."

Porsche and I looked at one another, then looked back at her. We were speechless.

Why do we stay in this abusive relationship with a country that doesn't want us if we can leave? I answered the question the same way I'm sure many Black Americans who have tasted the imperfect yet sweeter waters of other shores have answered.

"I don't know," I said honestly.

As we rode the train out of Amsterdam that next morning, I thought long on that question. Why do we stay? Why not start a life that expects a tomorrow, instead of just celebrating the miracle of still being here?

We didn't know then, but the idea of leaving America, or better yet escaping, would soon be in the forefront of many minds, as 2020 would become the year that a false empire was brought to its knees. Maybe my grandmother's wildest dream was that I would not be around when it happened.

2021

I've been thinking about this essay a great deal recently. I originally wrote it two years ago, after a trip to Europe in which I was left considering whether it was in the best interest of Black people to leave the United States if given the opportunity. I didn't want to update the essay because all my writing feels different to me since the pandemic took place and so many Black people were so publicly stolen from this world during 2020. So I suppose I felt it was best to keep a piece of my former self.

Let me first say that anti-Blackness exists in every country, which many people like to remind me when I bring up the prospect of Black Americans divesting from the United States. But I am hard-pressed to find many countries as systemically and socially steeped in the destruction of Black people as the US. The country was founded on principles and practices that consider and treat Black people as subhuman to this day. Though a great deal of gaslighting would lead many to believe that even though the US is far from perfect, we are better off here than somewhere else. Based on responses I've received to the questions I've posed on social media about Black people leaving the US it seems many agree with the idea that Black Americans are better off in this country than elsewhere.

But I understand how some could wonder how a country that doesn't provide basic human rights, such as healthcare or education, and basically refuses to have a conversation about reparations, could be the best place in the world.

Because white supremacy, capitalism, and the patriarchy literally raise us to not only tolerate, but to appreciate our pain and trauma.

I remember a Black man responded to one of my posts about potentially leaving the US and said, "A real Black man would stay and fight for his people." I wasn't mad that he said this, or at the implication that I am not a "real Black man" because I was raised the same way, taught that Black people are meant to struggle so that we might have anything. Black men specifically struggling helps build a "stronger" and "better" Black man.

When I think about this man's comments, I wonder two things: Does he realize how much of his opinion is rooted in white patriarchal structures? We are in the midst of the worst pandemic in modern history, which has disproportionately impacted Black people, yet the country refuses to do anything for us. Have his opinions changed or is he still focused on being a real Black man?

THE OPPRESSED MAY ALSO BE THE OPPRESSORS

"You have no idea what I've been through! How dare you tell me that I'm oppressive. Just because I'm white doesn't mean I don't go through things! Being Black is not more difficult than being a woman!"

—A woman who failed to realize people can be women *and* Black before calling her husband to arrest the Black guy who said something she didn't like

Oftentimes, there is a false narrative that white supremacy is upheld and perpetrated solely by white men. This narrative is largely based on the fact that white men own and operate the structures of white supremacy, as a result of the sexism and misogyny inherent within the patriarchy. Not only is this narrative false, but it creates added difficulty in trying to combat white supremacy itself. The reality is, just because white women don't have the utmost power in white supremacy doesn't mean they have none. There has been much discourse about white women upholding white supremacy since Minnesota police officer Kim Potter, a white woman, murdered Daunte Wright, an unarmed Black man, during a traffic stop. Some believe that her gender is unimportant in discussing the event, while others, such as myself, feel it's important to make the specific point that this act was committed by a white woman.

While some would argue that the patriarchy is as much of an oppressive force as white supremacy, history repeatedly proves this to be untrue. Consider the case of white suffragists such as Susan B. Anthony, who campaigned for white women's right to vote on the slogan "Woman First and Negro Last," understanding that white women's proximity to white men through the commonality of whiteness was more important to white men than Black men's commonality through gender.

Even now, many white women aim to uphold these systems, as was the case in their support for Donald Trump not only in 2016 but during 2020, when exit polls showed an increase in support for him by white women. This overt support of white supremacy isn't new amongst white women, as we saw with the suffragists and with the Daughters of the Confederacy and many other groups created by white women with the sole intent of upholding white supremacist ideology and structures.

Contrary to what many believe, upholding white supremacy also results from behaviors which are less overt, and not only by those considered "right-wing" or "conservative." Consider Amy Cooper, the white woman in Central Park who called the police on a Black bird-watcher named Christian Cooper. Mr. Cooper had done nothing but request that she place her dog on a leash, as park regulations required. In response, Amy Cooper said, "I'm going to tell [the police] an African American man is threatening my life." She then called the police and lied about the encounter, understanding that her whiteness gave her greater power within white supremacy than Christian Cooper had being a Black man within the patriarchy.

After the incident, Amy Cooper was referred to as a "Karen," which has become a pop culture term to represent instances in which white women have leveraged their power in white supremacy against those without such power, most often, against Black people. The issue with this term is that it inherently trivializes women's actions as a cultural phenomenon, or even a joke, as opposed to a manifestation of violent systemic white supremacy. It's hard to imagine Instagram pages such as "karensgoingwild," which is run by a white woman and man, being dedicated to mentally, physically, and emotionally violent acts committed against white women. The meme-ification of these incidents is yet another way the danger of white women's actions is obscured.

The problem of white supremacy isn't white men, it's whiteness. Which white women are absolutely a part of.

Whiteness has always been and continues to be the dominant source of power in America's systems, which is why white women within those systems have more power than everyone other than white men. White women have been conditioned to use their victimization within patriarchal structures as a tool to negate accountability for how they benefit from and perpetrate white supremacy. While they themselves may be drowning at times because of white men, they are responsible for everyone else sinking as well.

A GOOD WHITE WOMAN (I'M AN ALLY)

The young woman stood up and told them she had
something to say.

"White women who vote blue or red both consider
themselves well meaning while setting other people's lives
on fire."

A young white woman stood up immediately after.
She sighed, shook her head, and then nodded.

"I hear you. But—not me."

Wing-less chimera lost in Black phallus revelries
knowing tears
find me
gasping
in your father's prison.
Your husband's hell.
"Do you like white girls?"
The hair stands up on my neck,
like the book she pretended to read,
eyes on me in a sea of men she won't call her father on.
I'm only interested in making it,
where you can't fathom that I overcook rice,

stub my toe on the bed,

curse my mattress as if he pays rent,

laugh when they can't believe I kept that,

drink too much wine for my age,

cry for my mother when your father finds me,

home.

Fathers on vengeful steeds bearing

assumptions forged in lies,

I could have sworns,

I'm fairly sures,

of Jasmines and Lilies,

son's ghost setting the night ablaze.

Cursed weeping willows

damned to sand castles

doomed descendants hoist narrow shields

weighted down by the hollowness

of "Woman first and negro last."

Such haste to call upon your son's hell,

which became father's prison,

invisible hand you lent to build.

"There's an African American man near and I feel . . ."

As if you don't know who I am.

As if we don't have our special moments,

when you saw me and crossed the street,

clutched your pearls at the Sunken Place,

and your purse in the elevator when we met the day after,

gave me a sticker when I voted with you for your uncle Joe,

who won't stop your son from murdering my brother,
whose face you posted and books you read,
whose nose, lips, and hair you describe,
I tremble as you call your son
"threatened."

WHAT WHITE FEMINISM HAS TAKEN

PART 1: THE SHIELD

Some problems we share as women, some we do not. You fear your children will grow up to join the patriarchy and testify against you; we fear our children will be dragged from a car and shot down in the street, and you will turn your backs on the reasons they are dying.

—Audre Lorde

I was recently watching episodes of *The Twilight Zone* from the 1950s and I found myself reflecting on one of them for days after I finished it. The episode was about a white salesman, possibly in his sixties or seventies, who is visited by the human incarnation of death. The man is informed that his time with the living will soon come to an end by natural causes: "It's about time for your departure. You should feel lucky, many people don't receive a warning and time to get their affairs in order." The salesman is taken aback by this news, as I'm sure many people would be. The story line focuses on the man avoiding death by asking for more time to do something he's never done, which in turn makes death choose another person to "depart" with him as a replacement. Death chooses a young white girl who the salesman knew, so the salesman must then decide that he prefers to die so the white girl may live. Thanks to a clever plan and his skill set in keeping people engaged, the salesman is able to distract death, get to do the thing he's never done before dying, *and* save the girl.

A few things stood out and made me reflect on the episode. The first was that death was represented as a clean-cut white man in a suit, an image that to many would make death a palatable and non-frightening figure. But I actually found that image of death terrifying, as somewhere inside of me I've always believed my death would ultimately come from decisions made by a clean-cut white man in a suit or uniform. A judge, a corporate executive, a police officer, a politician, the clean-cut grim reapers of the Black community. The second thing that stood out to me was that the salesman was afforded the luxury to haggle over how and when he should die because he didn't feel fulfilled, though he was relatively old and had by his own account done many things in his life. I'm sure death also made himself known to many young Black people that week, and they were likely not afforded that same luxury.

The final thing I thought about, and maybe the most important thing in the context of this conversation, was the young white girl. While she was barely in the episode and was relegated to being a plot and character device, she symbolized something very true about our society. Unlike the salesman, the girl was not given the chance to live a full life, or to haggle for the opportunity to do so. Death, the clean-cut white man, seemed to find it appropriate to give that opportunity only to another white man. The girl is a mere bargaining chip, a life unequal, but one that will do. In that way, she is a symbol of how the benefits of the patriarchy are not afforded to white women and girls. Ultimately, her life is both put in jeopardy and saved by these white men without her ever realizing it. I highly doubt the salesman, born in the late 1800s or early 1900s, would have done the same thing had death chosen a young Black girl. It was likely the girl's whiteness that saved her life.

Some say that I'm overanalyzing the episode, but I truly believe that in many ways art and media provide mirrors for the realities of our world. Storytellers often reflect the world as they know it or want it to be. The production, cinematography, and direction of *The Twilight Zone* were all done by white men. While I can't speak for their worldviews, it doesn't surprise me that a group of white men would create an episode where a young white girl is both a potential sacrificial lamb and a representation of innocence and purity that should be saved. Which is likely why the other person death took couldn't be a Black or non-white child or adult. Besides the fact that there were few, if any, non-white actors in popular white-centered television programs at the time, the character who was being sacrificed had to be someone that a white man would be interested in saving. Much of society at that time, and now, has no problem sacrificing someone who isn't a white man for a white man's greater good. But only white girls and women generally captivate the interest and empathy of the white patriarchy enough to be saved and supported by it.

In many ways, that episode felt like a reflection of my own life. While the clean-cut white man in the suit or uniform may be the arbiter of my death, white women have always been the entities that have placed white men's gaze upon me. And that has been the case for many non-white people. The issue is that a white woman's power to victimize someone within white systems is juxtaposed with her own potential victimization at the hands of white men. For example, I spent much of my career working in the not-for-profit sector, where every single manager or president I had was a white woman.

Besides myself, there are many other men of color I know who have worked in the non-profit sector who often speak to the fact that white women can at times be just as, if not more, oppressive than the white men they've worked for in other sectors. They felt it was nearly impossible to hold the white women accountable for wrongdoings because more times than not, they weaponized their marginalization within the patriarchy against the marginalization of these men of color within white supremacy.

For example, some of these friends have spoken about white women who managed them, or had roles in executive leadership, flirting with them or asking them racially charged questions such as, "Where's the best hood to eat tacos in Queens?" Yet when they brought their issues with these interactions through channels such as human resources, nothing was done. In almost all cases, the power these women held in their roles within those institutions coupled with the power they held as white women in a white colonial settler society was too great to overcome.

It's those sorts of moments that led to my decision to leave the sector for my own well-being. As it often felt as though many of the white women I interacted with in the non-profit sector were less interested in dismantling white supremacist patriarchal systems to create more equity and equality for everyone as much as they were interested in attaining the position and power white men have historically held within said systems.

For any true dismantling or destruction of patriarchy and white supremacy to take place, we must all hold others and ourselves accountable for our roles in upholding them both. My hope is that this conversation will help white women reflect and make change, as I've asked men, and specifically Black men, to do the same.

I think you should start by talking about all of the white feminism that was protecting the women insurrectionists. That was a great example.

When insurrectionists stormed the US Capitol in the name of Donald Trump and white supremacy on January 6, 2021, I wasn't surprised as much as I was fearful. I feared for elected officials, and other human beings, such as Congresswoman Ayanna Pressley, who was forced to barricade herself in her office with her staff for their safety. I feared for the implications for future generations of seeing a Confederate flag swaying within the Capitol walls, and the sight of a noose hanging near the stairs to the Capitol entrance. These were images not of a backlash but rather of a whitelash at the idea that our country might have made some true progress. But what I feared the most, and what I expected to happen, was that there would be no accountability for the moment.

People often say our justice system is "broken" when events such as the Capitol insurrection or a police officer murdering a Black person unfold and there are insufficient or no criminal ramifications. But the reality is that our justice system, and all systems for that matter, is not broken—it is working for those it was intended to work for. I often think of the justice system, for instance, as a "just us" system, designed by and only truly meant to work for those benefiting from white supremacy and white patriarchy. There is the occasional mistake or strategic exception, but generally, most non-white men and women in America can attest to how exclusionary and stifling these systems often are.

Because white men have possessed the most power and visibility in these systems and moments such as the insurrection, white women's involvement and support is often lost to the echoes of time. White women have always played a large role in upholding and expanding white supremacy, as we saw during the insurrection, when many white women could be seen attacking the Capitol. One was even killed for attempting to break through a door that led to a room where elected officials were being protected.

Following the insurrection, there were abundant calls for accountability and references to the hypocrisy of how the insurrectionists, compared with those who marched for Black lives months earlier, were treated. There were also a few people, specifically non-white women, holding other white women accountable for their role in the insurrection, while most were blaming the moment solely on white men. But in response, many individual white women who identified as Democrats, and white feminist groups, pushed back. "This is white men's fault, we aren't going to blame women for this. They were coerced by those men."

These responses absolved white women of accountability for their actions as white people, as if they existed solely as women who are perpetual victims. The narcissism of white men in wanting to be the face of white supremacy has veiled white women's understanding that they too can be, and have been, white supremacists. In fact, white women in the early twentieth century created their own autonomous arm of the KKK, the Women of the Ku Klux Klan (WKKK), which had nearly half a million members. Daisy Douglas Barr headed the WKKK with several other women and promoted much of the same agenda as their male counterparts. One difference was the nuance with which they viewed the issues of immigration, segregation, and potential rights for Black and brown Americans. The WKKK saw other marginalized groups not just as abominations, but as threats to their own rights, as white women in the patriarchy. So, instead of combining forces with other marginalized groups against the white men who had amassed the full extent of power in America, they leaned into their whiteness and proximity to those men and made enemies of the other groups.

The WKKK also painted itself differently than did the KKK. Members of the WKKK drew in more members by referring to the group as a social club, organizing fundraisers, picnics, and baking events—when they weren't organizing cross burnings. This is the same conscious or unconscious palatability and respectability that mainstream white feminism adheres to today when committing acts of blatant or subtle bigotry. White supremacy and racist acts can't be *that* bad if the person who commits them also enjoys baking cookies—right?

In her own right, Daisy Douglas Barr also helped create the incarnations of white supremacy we see in the media today. She understood that to garner more support, white supremacy needed a makeover. Instead of focusing solely on hate, she wove in messaging about women's suffrage and was adamant against the use of racial slurs. Barr didn't believe in wearing Klan robes; she found them unsightly and lacking couth. Her bigotry was adopted by many because she positioned herself as a patriot and someone who cared about the well-being of white families and children in a world that was trying to make them obsolete. The goals of white supremacy are more attainable if the source is more relatable and acceptable.

But women didn't exist solely within the ranks of the WKKK, there were also those who worked directly with the KKK. Elizabeth Tyler was arguably one of the most influential individuals within the Klan in the early 1900s. She ran the KKK publicity team and helped modernize the group's messaging and platform. She understood two things. The first was the need to segment and diversify the Klan's platform, to make messaging that would resonate with groups in different parts of the country. For instance, a person living in an area with greater proximity to Asian people would receive marketing materials that spoke to how Asians were going to take jobs from white families. The second thing she understood was that the white patriarchy had stereotyped white women as being kind, soft, endearing, and needing to be saved, so if more white women were at the center of what the KKK was fighting for, then more white people would get involved.

Had it not been for Elizabeth Tyler, the KKK may have fallen apart. Ultimately, a white woman was able to help the Klan expand membership by broadening its scope of hatred. Mainstream white feminism's assumption that a white woman can't make an autonomous decision to help uphold a system she benefits from is inherently a patriarchal and anti-feminist view and results in white women's complicity in white supremacy. Discussing white women's role in white supremacy does not blame them for it, it holds them accountable for it.

Maybe some of them will understand the issue with the lawn signs.

I remember seeing a great many white women posting online that they had voted differently from their husbands, boyfriends, and other men in their lives during the 2016 election. Especially striking were the many photos circulating of people's lawns with signs in support of Donald Trump sitting next to signs in support of Hillary Clinton. What confused me was that many of these women spoke to how villainous Trump was in how he existed both within the patriarchy and within white supremacy. Some even called him "disgusting." But what I couldn't understand was how they could still actively choose to be with men who were supporting him.

Many white women seemingly had a way of ignoring the fact that their significant others voted for their oppression. Women claiming to be feminists, liberal, and progressive. Many women who voted in opposition to their significant others were praised for their "courage," which made no sense to me other than to indicate that a great deal of cognitive dissonance exists in that community. Even when white women have the power to force some level of accountability for the actions of white men, many opt out of doing so.

Whether they realize it or not, white women who don't hold the white men in their lives accountable for their actions are not only upholding the patriarchy, but fortifying it. I made a similar point on social media once, and many white women responded with various versions of the same sentiment: "I am not the men I choose to know or be with. They make their decisions and I make mine. Our relationships exist outside of those decisions." What a luxury it must be to have so much privilege that your relationship with a bigot may exist in a way that you don't feel yourself being crushed under the weight of their bigotry. Your boyfriend just voted to strip you of your reproductive rights and help further modern chattel slavery through the prison-industrial complex. But what does that matter if he looks really good in that Vineyard Vines shirt you love?

While we all have the power to hold individual views, we must also hold ourselves accountable for how our relationships with others legitimize the views and decisions of those we choose to be around. If bigotry isn't a deal breaker for you, then you are just as much of a bigot as the person you're refusing to step away from. And that refusal is rooted in both ignorance and entitlement.

Remember that message you got the other day? Oh, and the lady who was angry because you wouldn't appear for free?

But entitlement isn't solely a matter of not stepping away from or holding those around you accountable for bigotry; entitlement manifests in behaviors that may even seem simple on the surface. Last month I received 221 Instagram messages asking me questions and seeking advice about navigating racist family members and friends. Based on the photos of the people who sent these messages, five of them came from white men, one came from an Asian woman, and the rest were all from white women. The fact that such a large majority of the messages were coming from white women speaks to the entitlement they feel to my time and energy, all in the name of being progressive "allies."

This can also be found in the requests I receive to make appearances. I spend a great deal of my time publicly discussing a myriad of topics and giving thoughts on how we might work to combat these issues. I have the privilege of being invited to speak by companies, schools, and individuals, all of which are paid appearances, unless I designate otherwise for a specific reason. But since my debut book was released, I've been invited to appear in front of over twenty book clubs led by white women without so much as a mention of payment. I've turned down all of them. In one instance, I told the woman who messaged me why I was turning the opportunity down. Instead of offering to pay for the time of a bestselling author, she chastised me for wanting to be paid. As if I was somehow in the wrong and she was doing me a favor by asking me to spend my time talking to her and her friends.

I find it hard to believe that she would have thought it appropriate to chastise a white bestselling author who wanted to be paid for their time. This entitlement is rooted in not only how some white women view themselves, but how they consciously or unconsciously view the marginalized communities in their proximity. As if I should simply be happy to share space with white women, especially a group of them who have purchased my book.

So often, words such as "liberation" and "equality" ring hollow within white feminist rhetoric and theory because white women cannot see how they place their whiteness over them.

WHAT WHITE FEMINISM HAS TAKEN

PART 2: THE SWORD

Tell them about the Airbnb and the woman from Vice! That's a good one. Talk about that if it isn't too triggering.

One of the most mentally grueling and traumatic experiences of my life was at the hands of a white woman who was unable to see how these ideologies of patriarchy and white supremacy had conditioned and influenced her during the summer of 2020.

After having marched in the Black Lives Matter protests, having post-Covid syndrome, suffering the loss of family members and friends, and running a campaign to raise millions of dollars to help families in dire financial need during the pandemic, I was exhausted. As was my family. The mental, emotional, and physical toll that we had faced as Americans, and specifically Black Americans, was truly unfathomable. And this was all while a white supremacist was in the Oval Office. So, I decided I and my family needed some air.

I found a place on Airbnb that looked stunning. It was a small cabin with a large stream behind it in a seemingly private area. The perfect place for me, my fiancée, my eighteen-year-old cousin, and my eight-year-old brother to have a change of scenery for the first time in nearly six months. The drive to get there was about three hours, but I figured it was worth it. When we were a few miles from the property, we began to notice Trump flags on homes and street signs, but that is fairly common when you leave New York City, though still unnerving. We decided it was best to get to our Airbnb as soon as possible. When we arrived we noticed not only that the property was in a private area, but that there were no other houses within a ten-minute walk.

I left the car with my cousin to make sure the property was safe before my fiancée and little brother got out. We began seeing items that had not been in the photos online. There were photos of nude women with hexagrams tattooed on their chests and hands in one of the bedrooms, books about spells and paganism, statues of Baphomet, a taxidermy bird in a bag, drawing or carving on the basement floor that seemed like ritualistic iconography, a statuette of a dog inserting his penis inside a white woman from behind, and a myriad of other things that were unsettling and to me inappropriate for a child. My cousin agreed, as did my fiancée, who came into the house to give her own perspective and was terrified by the prospect of staying there.

I stood outside the cabin and called Airbnb to let them know about the situation and asked that they find us somewhere else to stay. Not simply because of the extensive iconography around the home, but also because it was unnerving that this material hadn't been in any of the listing's photos, as if it was placed there just before our arrival. Between that and the Trump flags nearby, I didn't feel comfortable staying there. Being Black in America for me has always meant considering the dangers of what may seem harmless to other people. I'm not personally religious and would have felt wary regardless of what the iconography all over the home was. We would have been just as uneasy with crucifixes and Bibles everywhere if they had not been advertised. Fanaticism of any kind has always been a marker of the depravities of white supremacy in my experience and learnings.

Airbnb spoke with the owner of the property, who offered to come and remove some of the items, and apparently told Airbnb this would take just a few minutes as "it was only a handful of things." Not only was this claim completely untrue, but I had no interest in these strangers being around my family. The host refused to issue a refund and Airbnb refused to help, as neither could understand why a Black family would feel uncomfortable in a space that wasn't as advertised and could feel dangerous. I also explained that because of the work I do and topics I discuss publicly, I often receive death threats and the home wasn't sitting right with us—to no avail. So we were forced to drive over three hours back to the city.

When we arrived home I decided to make a thread on Twitter chronicling the experience and mentioning Airbnb in hopes that public scrutiny would force them to issue me a refund. The thread included photos of the cabin and various items around it. The first post read: "We just drove three hours with my eight-year-old brother for a getaway and the house we arrived at ended up having seemingly satanic items and stuff for witchcraft rituals. We had to leave because my brother (and the rest of us) were frightened. But @Airbnb won't refund me. (THREAD)." The thread then detailed some of the experience (I forgot to include the Trump flags). Though at the time I had no idea what was required for a satanic ritual, I later found out that some of the items were in fact used in various rituals. But I want to make the point that I did not know whether the items were used for such practices at the time.

Airbnb contacted me within hours with an apology for the experience and a refund. Which I figured they would do, as brands often respect marginalized communities only when they are publicly held accountable by those with a platform. I found another Airbnb for us to drive to the next day and used my refunded money to pay for it. We spent two days away trying to clear our heads of the added stress from the events the day before. On the way back to the city, I received a call from a friend asking me if I had seen an article in *Vice News* about my Airbnb experience. I stopped the car and immediately pulled up the article, which was titled "We Talked to the Host Accused of Doing 'Satanic Rituals' in His Airbnb."

In the article the writer attempts to unravel the strings of what she frames as the result of my Christian delusion, which had victimized the Airbnb host and various communities who could be in danger of "satanic panic." She speaks with the host via a video call as he shows her around the home and apparently shows her the "handful" of items that were there. Obviously, a journalist wouldn't assume that a person who is trying to forward a narrative would possibly remove many of the aforementioned items. The writer says that I decided not to speak to Vice for the article when to my knowledge they had never contacted me. When I searched through my email I did find a message from her the day before that I had missed. In it she asked me to comment and said "I'm also—and I'm sorry if this is culturally or personally insensitive—curious what kind of harm you were concerned might befall you in the house? Do you have a religious objection to being in the presence of objects you consider to be Satanic?"

If given an opportunity to respond, I would have gladly explained that I'm not religious and that my concern was white supremacy and any form of white fanaticism. The fact of her asking a Black man what harm he thought might befall him in that house demonstrated her lack of thoughtfulness about the realities of some Black people's experiences in America. The writer also said that I had potentially put the Airbnb host in danger because I have a large platform (about 90,000 followers at the time), though I never mentioned the host by name, included any imagery of him, or gave the address of the property. Unlike what she did to a Black man she had never spoken to in an outlet that claims hundreds of millions of readers. The article drew the ire of thousands of people who attacked me on social media and in email, especially after it was shared by the Church of Satan and covered by other white writers in outlets such as *Forbes*. All of this seemed to have some connection to the writer at *Vice*.

My fiancée decided to do some research on the writer and found that she was a fan of iconography similar to what we had found in the home. I decided to write a thread in response, explaining how her problematic, one-sided, and borderline racist article was written in an echo chamber of not only her whiteness but also her personal interests.

The thread received a great deal of support from non-white people who could understand my perspective. But my platform was outmatched by the platforms of those dissenting, most of whom were white and identified as politically leftist, giving them the opinion that they were in a position to undermine my perspective as a Black man and tell me the experience was not about race. One person who is very popular in leftist Twitter spaces and has about 500,000 followers called me a "clown" and continued to berate me about the experience. At one point he even referred to me as a "Karen," completely missing the fact that this name had been given to white women committing racially charged acts.

The experience became so overwhelming I stopped using Twitter for weeks because I couldn't post anything without being trolled. I also began using another email account because people were flooding my primary email with messages stating that I was "race baiting" and "grifting."

Keep going, it's okay. I know it hurts, but this is important.

I posted a few videos and screenshots of responses from Black people attempting to explain how some Black people might feel in the situation, but the more I did, the more prominent white writers and social media personalities told me I was weaponizing race and being problematic. I was being gaslighted by white people, and primarily white women, over an article written by a white woman with either an agenda or a massively biased gap in her lens as a writer. But it didn't matter, as is often the case for non-white people when white people decide they aren't interested in listening or have a vested interest in invalidating. This is especially true of those who can weaponize their own marginalization while possessing more power than the person they are victimizing.

Understanding how a Black family may feel they are in peril because a white person conducts themselves in any way that seems odd should not be a surprise or an enigma in a country where millions of people are marching for Black people not to be murdered while simply doing things such as jogging or sleeping. But whiteness is louder and more insulated, and it ultimately won the day because white men and white women who claim to care about Black lives can't think beyond their ingrained white supremacy.

Many people believe that political alignments absolve them of committing bigoted acts or having bigoted views. This is why I've always felt white people who are in leftist, liberal, and progressive spaces can be more dangerous than overt white supremacists. I'd rather we both know you hate me so I may avoid you, as opposed to you telling me you don't hate me while hurting me and then telling me I'm lying about it.

Maybe you should talk to them about the book. Maybe that will help them understand if they don't already?

Another example of the power and privilege some white women possess is on full display in the extremely white publishing industry. How white, you ask? Well, according to the *New York Times*, only 11 percent of books in 2018 were written by people of color, 85 percent of editors at the four major publishing houses are white, and of that number 74 percent are women. This means that most modern American literature exists within an echo chamber of white women. It also means that most of American literature comes with the baggage of whatever ideologies, conditioning, preconceived notions, and interests those white women have. Thus readers and critics are not only engaging with books that are primarily white, they are also likely conditioned in their tastes and interests by that very fact. Good writing, enjoyable writing, notable writing is primarily gauged through a lens of whiteness.

I learned the hard way just how white-woman-centric the industry was when my debut book, *The Black Friend*, was released in December 2020. The book was well received and instantly made the *New York Times* bestseller list for young adult nonfiction. In my excitement about the sales of the book, I decided to read some of the reviews from the public (never do this). While many of them were very good, a few negative ones stood out to me, because of both what they said and who was saying it.

The negative reviews were all primarily by white women, and many weren't so much about what I had written, as about who had written it. I remember two reviews in particular. One said, "The entire book feels like he's mansplaining. It should have been written by a Black woman." She gave me three stars on a book that was intended to explain things to young readers. Another review said, "He's only talking about what people did to him. What about what he did to others as a male in society?" That person gave two stars to a book about a Black boy growing up in America facing racism. A boy who in much of the book was in elementary school.

To help me understand how some white women critically, or not so critically, view writing, I decided to read white women's critiques of Toni Morrison's Pulitzer Prize–winning book, *Beloved*. Reading the negative reviews of the work of this recipient of the Nobel Prize in Literature both frustrated me for her and eased my feeling of weight about my own reviews. I remember one review by a poster who appeared in her photo to be a white woman. She said, "I tried to get into it. But everything feels so exaggerated in the experiences. I can't relate like I want to." The white woman who felt like a Black woman was exaggerating the devastation of being Black in America, especially during slavery, and couldn't relate to the stories of Black women fighting for survival gave the book three stars.

That comment revealed something to me that I will remember until the day I set my pen down for good. For a non-white creative, in many parts of the world, success and talent are measured through a white lens, which at best doesn't truly understand you and at worst is consciously or subconsciously prejudiced toward you.

Which is why it's important for non-white people to measure our success in the mirror.

I have the constant understanding that the critiquing, reading, and potential acquisition of my work will always run primarily through a filter of white women. If those white women are not thoughtful about their own whiteness and conditioning within oppressive systems they benefit from, then non-white writers such as me face a nearly impossible battle. A battle that extends into every facet of our lives, all the details of our daily experiences in which white women are causing harm with their power but largely refusing to be accountable for their harm. Clinging solely to the violence they've endured while ignoring the violence they perpetrate.

While they don't hold all the cards, white women most certainly are playing a hand. That hand either helps dismantle oppression for everyone or simultaneously upholds patriarchy and white supremacy, intentionally or not.

BUILDING ANEW

THERAPY (HOW DO YOU FEEL?)

Learning to acknowledge and talk about it wasn't something he was doing for himself. It was something he was doing for everyone around him.

Does anyone hear that?
The sound of sweat rolling down my brow.
I am someone who once had a body
numbers on a ledger
where there was once a name
orphans singin' about a mother
none of us have met
foster parents don't want our names
just our numbers, our hands, our feet, our shame
in the middle of the night
just the sounds of my sister
but when it was my brother's turn
the ledger man made me watch
then he gave me something to cry about
in front of her who was meant to be my kin
tears of joy that he didn't do it to her
but she couldn't look at me the same
all I wedded was my number.

What's that sound?

The thumping of my heart

demanding to leave my chest.

I am a squatter in a body that was never mine

flesh birthed of expectations and failed

promises to these bones

may my fractures make me more

or less than them

but momma I wanna sing

and daddy I wanna dance

this head that was never mine is lowered

from my dreams to my realities

lip and eye on loan are split and blackened

boys like that . . .

boys like that . . .

your grandma would roll in her grave

don't forget you just squattin', boy!

It's so loud!

Screeching of pen to pad noting

these foreign tears.

I am a bottle floating in a storm

named after my nameless parents

filled with postcards sent from

the agony of bodiless people

but I find land that wants me to call it home

home doesn't know I am filled with agony

and all I've ever seen is the storm

the thunder, the lightning, the wind, all that's left

is the seed which was under the house
that is no longer wanting to be called home
a seed becomes a tree standing firm in the wind
but it only knows storms
so it does what storms do.
It's quieter today.
The silence of someone listening.

WHAT WAS MADE, MAY BE BROKEN

He told the readers: Patriarchy has a beginning and, as a result, can have an end. As we must imagine and plot the course of history in how it came to be, we must have bolder imaginations in plotting to dismantle it.

Patriarchy,

I fear that once it is time for you to meet your demise, it will have been a great while since I closed my eyes. As will be the case with everything that should be destroyed that has left my people undone. Nevertheless, my eyes are open now, seeing the truth.

As the sun rose on your time, it too shall set. The marriage of fire and courage has toppled every empire in its path—I pray my words serve to give our village both. Though none can say how old you are, you are not as old as you seem. Not so old that when I'm finally home the ancestors won't be able to tell me about a time before you. About how you cut your way through with the sword of capitalism and shielded yourself from our arrows with oppressive tales.

I hope these words echo in the stead of your eulogy. Although we may not all know it yet—no one will miss you. Women will rise, binaries will crumble, identity will flourish, and the meek will in fact inherit the earth. There will be dancing as there has *never been dancing before, a celebration scored with all the songs you've stolen. My mother's song, her mother's song, her father's song, and my song.*

But I'm singing now, knowing I am the ancestor of free un-colonized people.

My children will bask in divine femininity and masculinity knowing they may live equally in their bodies, and those bodies may be called whatever they desire. The symbols and stereotypes of your myths, fables, and lies will shrink back to the nothingness from which they came. We will reject the conspiracies you've injected into the veins of my brothers telling them what "makes them a man." We will extinguish the cowardice that has created a culture of our Black trans sisters fighting for survival.

Tomorrow will take a sledgehammer to the institutions of yesterday that have kept the most marginalized from power that was never meant solely for men. Where there were once divisions founded in hierarchy, dichotomy, and mentality there will be courage. Through the enlightenment of intersectionality we will move these mountains of caste, until equity is not a dream, but rather a standard.

There is a shared imagination for more than you have given us, something more than this for our descendants. It will take collective consciousness and courage which is still a seed, but that is where all life begins. The seed of an idea gives birth to revolution, which is the mother of progress and liberation.

I can hear a heartbeat, and it's becoming stronger with every person who reads this notice of your impending doom. The pulse of change grows louder with every person who decides to imagine something more than the patriarchy and its binaries, shackles, and violence.

That pulse is the rhythm of our ancestors' songs we are reclaiming. The songs of the women the world refused to hear, the transgender children that families didn't want to see, the gender-nonconforming parents that friends wouldn't try to understand, the boys and girls losing themselves to someone else's standards, and all of those who have been oppressed under the patriarchy.

These words are for them. This is their song. I hear their lyrics as clearly as I've heard anything in my life. Do you hear it?

They say "we will be free."

Sincerely,
Fire and Courage

IN THAT DIRTY MIRROR

So they wiped away furiously
in an attempt to reveal something
less toxic. Something—better.

Covered in steam from the showers
that were supposed to wash away the rain.

Where the parts of you you're trying to forget
and the parts of you you're to remember
can catch up like old friends.

With shaking index finger, you write
"I am still here."

A reminder that you are more than the list
of people you couldn't, shouldn't, and wouldn't be.

As you watch the scuffs on your knees heal
from begging bad religions to believe in you.

It's here that your compass begins to point away from your pain
and back to your name.

Through smears on subjective glass, the bags under your eyes
hold the seeds that will become the fruits of your labor

and the flowers given to celebrate your joy.

In this reflection may you learn to be
gracious with yourself.

IN THE END (LETTING GO OF OUR FATHERS)

To the father I've never known:

People tell me I look just like my mother, so much so, they assume she's my sister. This has always felt like a gift, something of divine favor. When I look in the mirror I am not reminded of a stranger. I can think of few things more heartbreaking than a child who doesn't know their parent's face. This is the face of the woman who chose me. The face of the woman who gave me a chance.

So much time has passed since I last considered the mystery of your face. Nearly as much time as it took me to feel comfortable living with this name—someone else's name. Though I no longer consider this to be your name, nor our name, but rather my name. The legacy of the man who wears the crown of this name will not be one of walking away.

But I did consider your face for a long time, especially while chasing ghosts to ask why I wasn't good enough. Haunted by fantasies of what expressions you might make if you were proud of me, how stern your voice might become if you were disappointed, and how you might make me smile when reminding me of my worth in a world where so many others lie to me about it. Eventually I began to believe that fatherhood was nothing more than a fairy tale for children. I believed what the world told me I was and what the world told me

I was supposed to be. I was a Black boy who couldn't find the love I wanted, I settled for the hatred they make accessible to us. The voids left by your ghosts became filled with the sins of my own demons.

For so long, I couldn't bear to look in a mirror, knowing it was not just my mother's face I would see. My reflection was filled with the faces of all of the women who had been deceived into knowing my demons. Faces with eyes that saw something in me I could not see in myself, ears that heard nothing but lies, and mouths that spoke of sorrow as I walked away from them and toward my own selfishness. That mirror would have shown me a young man who thought his pain and trauma entitled him to cause others pain and trauma. In that way, I suppose you and I do share a resemblance.

A person who doesn't know how to love themselves can never truly love anyone else. It's a lesson I didn't learn until I began seeing gray in my beard, long after I had lost myself and found myself more times than I care to say. A lesson for broken boys who need a path so they don't have to become broken men. This was a lesson not offered to me at eight years old let alone at twenty-eight, so I'm sure it was not offered to you at eighteen. Such a tender age for a boy to decide whether he was going to become a father. But I do wonder whether the men who decide not to be fathers consider how those pieces are left to be picked up by the women who decide to be mothers.

Did you consider whether I was going to learn to tie a tie for my first internship from my college roommate, whose father taught him? Did you consider whether I was going to have to become the man of the house much younger than you were when you decided to leave? Did you consider how I was going to explain to the other kids at camp why I stayed in my room and pretended to be sick when they *had father and son weekend? Did you consider that the same world that was rigged against you was also rigged against me? Did you consider how long it would take me to realize that I didn't ask to be born and none of this was my fault?*

The thing about life is that every new day you have is an opportunity to choose to be someone different—someone better. I can't judge the boy who made mistakes, as I've made a lifetime of them myself, and I expect to make many more. But I do judge the man who refuses to atone for what his younger self has done.

At some point, whether that's in this life or the next, we all have to look in the mirror. I chose to look during this life, and when I did I loathed what I saw. But I had the courage to begin changing. I say begin, because it's a process. I aim to be a better man today than I was yesterday, and a better man tomorrow than I was today. Doing so has allowed me the gift of my relationship with my fiancée. We came into each other's lives imperfect, and as such we don't expect perfection in our relationship, but we try for each other. We try to be stronger, we try to be more vulnerable, we try to be more patient, we try to be better. I'm learning that love is sometimes as simple as not running away from the hard parts.

I think the most difficult part of change is accepting that you are not innocent. Truly being accountable to what you once were is understanding that some people may not forgive you, and that's fine. They deserve that. You don't change to be forgiven, you change so that there might be fewer people tomorrow who have to decide whether to forgive you.

But, if someone does forgive you, know that it's actually for them and not you. Having a place in your heart reserved for anger or hatred only takes up space that could be used for something that actually serves you. Something beautiful and joyful. Which is why if I were to become an ancestor today, I would do so having forgiven you for not being the man you never found the courage to become. My heart and my mind will never forget what you have done, but I'm releasing myself from you. What was once pain will now be a lesson, so that I may one day be a monument to the fathers and husbands I never knew.

I have to believe that you will find the courage to become something more than what you have been. Not for me, or the other people you've possibly hurt, but for yourself. If I don't truly believe that you can be better, then I am lying when I say it is actually possible.

I forgive you for not being there for a hard life that made me harder. I forgive you for making me wonder whether that was you in a crowd of men I wished were there to pick me up after school. I forgive you for not having the lessons to teach that I will one day teach my children, and hopefully someone reading this book. I forgive you for not knowing the man I'm becoming, and the boy who stumbled and fell to get here.

This is me letting you go now, in hopes that I may continue to find healing in a world that so often teaches us what we aren't. May we be brave enough to look in the mirror and find out not just what we are—but what we may become.

In hopes that you find your shore,
Fred

ACKNOWLEDGMENTS

To Porsche, who stands on the sky with me.

To my mother, may we one day get it right. In this life or the next.

To my grandmother, who like far too many Black women, found love to pour into others despite how little was poured into her.

To Sarah, who saw the vision and took this journey with me.

To Kaylan, who reminds me just how high a tree can grow if it wants to.

To George, who opened my eyes to so much all those years ago.

To Mikki Kendall, Angela Davis, bell hooks, Alice Walker, Audre Lorde, Patricia Hill Collins, Kimberlé Williams Crenshaw, Moya Bailey, and the countless Black feminist and womanist writers and theorists I've learned from.

To Black people around the world, I love you.

To my readers, who have given me the opportunity to help play a part in something much bigger than myself.

BIBLIOGRAPHY

Amnesty International. "It's Intersex Awareness Day—Here Are 5 Myths We Need to Shatter." *Amnesty International*, October 26, 2018.

Bates, Lydia. "Patriarchal Violence: Misogyny from the Far Right to the Mainstream." Southern Poverty Law Center, February 1, 2021, https://www.splcenter.org/news/2021/02/01/patriarchal-violence -misogyny-far-right-mainstream.

Fisher, Robert B. *West African Religious Traditions: Focus on the Akan of Ghana (Faith Meets Faith)*. Orbis Books, 1998.

Images, Highway Patrol. "Police Officers." *Data USA*, 2019, datausa .io/profile/soc/police-officers.

Lee & Low Books. "Where Is the Diversity in Publishing? The 2019 Diversity Baseline Survey Results." *Lee & Low Books* blog, February 10, 2020, blog.leeandlow.com/2020/01/28/2019diversity baselinesurvey.

Moss, Emily, Kriston McIntosh, Wendy Edelberg, and Kristen Broady. "The Black-White Wealth Gap Left Black Households More Vulnerable." *Brookings*, December 8, 2020, www.brookings .edu/blog/up-front/2020/12/08/the-black-white-wealth-gap-left -black-households-more-vulnerable.

Mowat, Chris. "Don't Be a Drag, Just Be a Priest: The Clothing and Identity of the Galli of Cybele in the Roman Republic and Empire."

Wiley Online Library, July 1, 2021, onlinelibrary.wiley.com/doi
/full/10.1111/1468–0424.12518.

Petersen, Emily. "Racial/Ethnic Disparities in Pregnancy-Related
Deaths . . ." Centers for Disease Control and Prevention, September 6,
2019, www.cdc.gov/mmwr/volumes/68/wr/mm6835a3.htm?s_cid
=mm6835a3_w.

So, Richard Jean. *Redlining Culture: A Data History of Racial Inequality and Postwar Fiction*. Columbia University Press, 2020.

"The Trevor Project National Survey 2020," www.thetrevorproject
.org/survey-2020/?section=Introduction.

ABOUT THE AUTHOR

FREDERICK JOSEPH is the *New York Times* bestselling author of *The Black Friend* and an award-winning marketing professional, activist, and educator. He has won the Comic-Con Humanitarian of the Year Award and was chosen for *The Root* 100 List of Most Influential African Americans. He was recently featured on the *Forbes* 30 Under 30 List. He lives in Long Island City, New York.